AARON C[ARTER]

AN INCOMPLE[TE] [ST]O[R]Y
OF AN INCOMPLETE [LIFE]

**ANDY
SYMONDS**
and
AARON CARTER

Ballast Books

Ballast Books, LLC

Copyright © 2022 by Andy Symonds

All rights reserved. No part of this book may be reproduced in any form or by any electronic or mechanical means, including information storage and retrieval systems, without permission in writing from the publisher or author, except by reviewers, who may quote brief passages in a review.

ISBN 978-1-955026-53-6

Printed in the United States

Published by Ballast Books
www.ballastbooks.com

For more information, bulk orders, appearances or speaking requests, please email info@ballastbooks.com

DEDICATION

This book, though incomplete, is dedicated to Aaron Carter. Though your life, too, was incomplete, I hope you know how many lives you touched during your time here.

Rest in peace.

AUTHOR'S NOTE

November 7, 2022

Most of the material in this book came from a series of interviews between me and Aaron Carter in 2019 and 2020. We met in person three times for a total of about eighteen hours, spoke on the phone sporadically over a couple of years, and communicated regularly via text about Aaron's life, hopes, dreams, and demons. Our plan was to finish writing his autobiography and publish it shortly thereafter.

Work went slow. It could be difficult to get ahold of Aaron, and the project endured many starts and stops. In 2020, when Aaron told me he was finally healthy and wanted to focus more on the book, my schedule wouldn't permit another project at that time. I offered to have another one of my writers work with him on more interviews, but he said he only trusted me to tell his story. I was and am honored by his faith and trust in me.

But we did get a lot of work done in those couple of years, even if it was erratic. When Aaron and I were able to sit down for interviews, he was always thoughtful, honest (as far as I could tell), self-aware, and open with me. He had a boy-like quality to him, an innocence despite being far from innocent. I could see hurt in his eyes, pain that he masked with jokes, bravado, marijuana, and whatever else he may or may not have been ingesting outside of my eyesight. He shared with me that his main substance issues were with Xanax and huffing canned air like Dust Off, but while we got most of the work done in the spring and summer of 2019, he said he wasn't doing either of those. As we now know, he never was able to defeat those foes.

Normally, when I'm ghostwriting someone's book, they tell me their story, and I record the interview while taking notes. I then write a chapter while constantly peppering them with clarifying questions: "What did the sky look like? How did the house smell? Was this before or after you moved to Florida?" Then, when the chapter is done, I review it with the author, ensuring all details are accurate and to the best of their recollection. I then edit and rewrite based on that review so the chapter reads exactly as the author envisioned it. I do very little fact-checking or research independent of the author's recollection (aside from names, dates, and other clear-cut "facts")—by definition, an autobiography is the subject's own recall of his or her life, and everyone remembers life events differently. That is part of the beauty of reading someone's recount of their own life: It's simply their interpretation of the past, present, and future. Autobiographies are the recollections of the subject, in their own words—nothing else. More so than most, I think that's what this book represents.

Sadly, Aaron and I will never finish that process. I can't review any more chapters with him or ask clarifying questions. The rest of the book comprises my notes from our conversations, mostly Aaron's stream of consciousness as he spoke it to me, verbatim. These are notes I took as we conducted our interviews, cleaned up and edited the best I could without losing any context or meaning. In some cases, when it wasn't clear what or who Aaron was referring to, rather than make an educated guess as to his meaning, I either omitted the comment/story or left my own notes referencing possible confusion. Likewise, I decided to leave the notes I included in otherwise completed drafts for Aaron to later qualify. Now that he cannot do that, I feel it's only right to leave those unanswered questions for the reader to ponder.

The Aaron that I knew was friendly, personable, kind, and gentle. I can't imagine him wanting to hurt so much as a fly. I know that he carried a lot of pain because of how he grew up and the relationship (or lack thereof) with his family, but I know he carried a lot of love too. Hell, that's what he named his final album and had tattooed across his neck.

I know how excited Aaron was about this book and how he wanted the world to finally understand him. I remember when my wife and I went to see him in concert in Huntington, NY, he pointed me out in the crowd and giddily told the audience how revealing his book was going to be and that he couldn't wait for it to come out. I hope that by releasing it now, it will give him some peace.

That's all Aaron ever wanted.

PROLOGUE

March 30, 2019

As I wound my rental car though the mountains, the heat seemed to grow more oppressive as the elevation climbed. I was driving a crappy economy sedan, and the car groaned under the burden of the blasting air conditioning and steep incline. Along the edges of the highway, the jagged scenery consisted mostly of sand, rock, scrubs, and the occasional lonely house, usually standing alone stoically as if daring someone to approach it. Something told me those inhabitants just wanted to be left alone.

By the time I finally reached the town limits of Lancaster, which conjured images of a post-gold rush ghost town, I was starving. Aaron had just texted me to say that he was running late for our meeting, so I knew I had time to kill. I drove the few lonely, dilapidated blocks that I assumed was Lancaster's version of downtown and ate half of a terrible salad from a diner. Then, I waited.

I was used to it. I'd been working with Aaron Carter on his book for about a month, and waiting had been the norm. Most scheduled calls got delayed if not pushed altogether. Aaron was always very polite and apologetic about the miscues and ALWAYS had a very good reason for them.

Once, after a dentist appointment, I got a text: "My mouth is literally closed shut we're gonna have to do tomorrow," with a corresponding selfie showing what looked like costume blood covering his lips and running down his chin. "They fucked me up," he wrote under the photo. Another time, it was: "Hey brotha so sorry been with family haven't even had phone on."

Today, he was late for our first meeting in person, at his house, because he was meeting his baby niece for the first time. I could forgive that—I hadn't known Aaron long, but I already understood how important family was to him. He talked incessantly about the love he had for his siblings and parents, though I hadn't yet had a chance to ask him about his current relationship with them.

Earlier that afternoon, after landing at LAX, I had confirmed (again) our appointment. "Hey man, just landed. How's your day going?" I texted him.

"Pretty good just with the family. Seeing this one. For the first time," he wrote, then included an adorable picture of a chubby baby girl. It was captioned, "Goooooood morning harper &babe." (I sent him a picture of my then one-and-a-half-year-old daughter. "Omg soo cute haha" was his response.)

Harper was his twin sister Angel's kid. Aaron was beyond excited to meet her and was still at the beach in Malibu visiting. I would happily wait for him outside his house if it meant he got to spend more time with his family.

At 10:09 p.m., he finally texted, "pulling up now." We shook hands and went inside to get to work.

We worked most of that night. I got the impression Aaron didn't usually go to bed until the sun was up. Aaron and his girlfriend at the time, Lina, were incredibly gracious and made me feel at home. His house was nice, though not world famous boy band nice. It was clean and sparsely furnished with a huge, comfy couch directed at a big-screen TV. We sat down on the couch while a bowl, at least a quarter ounce of weed, several rolled blunts, two packs of cigarettes (menthols, if I remember correctly), and several lighters were never out of arm's reach.

We talked about a lot that night. I forget what time we quit and I started the long drive back to my in-laws' house in Hermosa Beach, but my eyes burned with exhaustion and my brain was fried. He'd revealed a lot in those hours together, and my mind wouldn't shut down. I was already processing how best to tell his story.

Because it was a hell of story, that much was clear.

TABLE OF CONTENTS

Chapter 1: 9/11	1
Chapter 2: Meet the Carters	10
Chapter 3: My Idol	17
Chapter 4: I Got the Bug	27
Chapter 5: A Star Is Born	35
Chapter 6: Neverland	39

AARON'S THOUGHTS

On His Relationship with Michael Jackson	58
On Getting His Start in Music	60
On His Crazy Schedule as a Child	61
On Money	65
On His Albums	66
On Moving	72
On Supporting His Family Financially	73
On Girls	76
On His Parents	77
On Drugs	81

The Keys	83
On Nick and the Backstreet Boys	87
On Going Back to Work	89
On Turning Eighteen	91
Los Angeles	94
Orlando	98
Miami	103
Back to Orlando	105
New York	109
On His Mental Health	112

Chapter 1
9/11

It was a wonderful day to be a famous teenager in New York City.

I remember getting up early that morning—early, at least, for a thirteen-year-old coming off a historic performance at Madison Square Garden. But as I stood at my window in the W, looking into a bright blue sky, my excitement wasn't residual adrenaline from opening for Michael Jackson and singing in front of 35,000 people the night before. I was already used to that. No, what had caused me to get out of bed before the sun was fully over the Manhattan skyline was an invitation from Michael—or Dookie, as I would come to call him—to fly on his private jet to visit an amusement park in Minnesota.

Yesterday's concert had been a celebration of the thirtieth anniversary of the Jackson 5, a star-studded tribute widely lauded as one of the biggest music events of the year. It was the first time all the Jackson brothers had performed together in seventeen years (it wasn't technically the Jackson 5 because all six brothers participated), and I had performed alongside artists like Usher, Luther Vandross, Whitney Houston, and 98 Degrees. Elizabeth Taylor had introduced the Jacksons, with Chris Tucker doing the honors for Michael. Liza Minelli sang "Over the Rainbow," and Gladys Knight performed "I Heard It Through the Grapevine" for the capacity crowd. (Almost thirty million more would watch the CBS broadcast in November.) Tickets had been going for as high as $20,000, and the audience was a who's who of New York aristocracy. It had been an amazing night of love and happiness that I was honored to be a part of but was not intimidated by. I knew I belonged on the stage with those performers. And Michael knew it too.

 I had already broken his record for the youngest artist to have four songs in the Billboard top ten. My brother Nick was in the biggest boy band on the planet, and I myself had already sold millions of albums, been on hit television shows and movies, and performed in packed arenas around the world. My close friends included Lindsay Lohan, Bruce Willis and Demi Moore (who hired me to perform at Rumer's sixteenth birthday party), Queen Latifah, Will Smith, and Justin Timberlake. No, I was not intimidated in the least.

My parents and I had flown to New York from our home in Florida the day before the show. We did the normal New York touristy stuff, visiting [*what*], but none of it resonated with me. Back then, I had no appreciation for the significance of the venues I played or cities we visited. It was just another gig, something I had already done thousands of times. I conducted my standard rehearsal with my dancers that afternoon and attempted to nap. Then, it was showtime. I knew the MSG performance would be a cakewalk for me.

Even so, I remember being especially exhausted—to the point of barely being able to stand when it was time to leave for the venue. But that was normal for me; I was tired all the time as a kid. My parents kept my schedule intense with constant touring, appearances, and interviews with barely a break. I worked around the clock my entire childhood. I still feel like I'm trying to catch up on sleep from back then. But I was used to the exhaustion, and the show went great. Michael watched my whole performance from the side of the stage.

Afterward, he approached me backstage. No managers, no bodyguards, just a super warm, loving guy congratulating me on a great performance. I remember thinking, *He's so nice.* Michael smiled his shy, almost embarrassed smile as if he didn't want me to see it and said, "Aaron, that was amazing! You're going to follow in my footsteps someday, I know it! You're the only one who can do all the things I did. Mark my words, you'll be taking over my spot one day."

It was a powerful statement coming from the King of Pop. Surreal but music to my ears, though I don't know if the significance of what he said to me sank in that day.

After that show, we became close. We'd have many similar conversations over the years, and he always made it clear he believed I was his heir apparent. It took a while for the impact of Michael's generosity to hit me, but eventually, it did. Now, when I meet young singers, I encourage them just like he did for me. And I always tell their parents to pay their taxes.

I don't think Michael had ever met anyone he thought capable of carrying his torch. It made sense that we were such kindred spirits; we had each gone through the exact same things at such a young age. Adults pulling us in so many directions. Our families relying on us for their income. Not knowing who to trust. Michael understood what was going on in my life like no one else could because he had been through it. He had forged the path that I was on. And he saw a lot of himself in me.

But that day, I just told him, "Cool," and asked if I could have the jacket he had worn during his performance.

That was where my head was at as a pampered, entitled, thirteen-year-old used to ordering adults around and getting whatever I wanted. It was a white military-style jacket studded with Swarovski crystals, and I thought it was the coolest thing I'd ever seen. He smiled softly, telling me, "One day." Then, he asked if I'd like to fly to Minnesota with him and Macaulay Culkin in the morning.

My parents agreed, as long as my tutor, Mark Giovi; tour manager, Ron Jakeway; and bodyguard, Richard Rodriguez, went with me. It was decided that we would leave in the morning with Michael while my parents headed back to Florida. We finished media and fan obligations, then went back to the hotel.

After finishing my fruit and oatmeal the morning after the concert, I headed to the lobby where a limo was waiting. I was very close to my parents at the time and always had a hard time leaving them. Once we completed our teary goodbyes, they headed to LaGuardia, and I got in the limo for Teterboro Airport, a smaller private airport in New Jersey where Michael had his jet.

The limo headed out of Manhattan. Suddenly, the car began to shake, and the jarring movement was followed by a loud, flopping sound vibrating from outside. We had blown a tire, forcing the driver to pull over on the side of the busy highway. Just before he reached the shoulder, I saw a semi barreling toward us. At the last minute, the truck just barely was able to swerve, narrowly missing us and avoiding crushing the limo.

"Holy shit," we all said as the car came to a stop next to the Hudson River. We piled out, happy to be alive, while our driver started to make arrangements to get the tire fixed. Then, we waited.

I had been to New York dozens of times but had never really taken the time to appreciate the scenery. As I said, my life was *Groundhog Day* back then. Same performance, new city/arena. But that day, for some reason, I stood there admiring the skyscrapers across the river as we waited, staring at the World Trade Center jutting high above them all. I remember laughing to myself, thinking about the buildings' role in *Home Alone*. And to think, today I would be flying on a private jet with Macaulay Culkin.

Twenty or thirty minutes went by, and the tire still wasn't changed. Mark, Richard, and Ron were trying to help the driver, but they were having problems. All of a sudden, there was a roar overhead. I looked up and saw this huge plane flying right above us, so low that I could read the letters and numbers on its underside.

"That plane is going to crash!" I yelled to everyone standing on the shoulder. They all looked up and saw the plane bank left, then hard right. We had a direct line of site and watched it slam directly into the World Trade Center. It wasn't until three seconds later that we heard the impact. It sounded like someone clapping two-by-fours together. We all froze in shock at what we had just witnessed.

Then, I realized my parents were at the airport. I was convinced that they had been on that plane and was soon out of my mind with fear. When I frantically tried calling them, I got an error message that I had never heard before. Cell phones weren't working. There was no way to get through.

"Forget Teterboro airport," I pleaded with the limo driver. "Take me to LaGuardia. I have to find my parents!"

Everyone jumped back in the car, and the driver sped toward the airport. [*When did the tire get fixed?*] It would be the longest drive of my life. We turned the television on in the limo to see if we could figure out what had happened.

A breaking newscast cut it in. "I told you!" I said. "It *was* a commercial plane!" The guys hadn't believed me, thinking that it had to have been pilot error with a small private plane. But they hadn't seen the plane until it had already passed us. I had seen it. I knew what it was.

As we were discussing the odds of a commercial aircraft crashing directly into a skyscraper, we watched the television in horror as the second plane hit. Now, we knew for sure that it was terrorism.

When we reached LaGuardia, the entrance was in chaos. Mayhem. Cars were parked everywhere, people panicking and pouring out of the airport. There was the feeling of a near riot. We got as close as we could to the main entrance. Then, I climbed onto the limo's roof, screaming, "Jane Carter! Bob Carter!" over and over. After a while, miraculously, I saw my parents running toward me. My dad reached me first and scooped me up, asking if I was okay.

"I'm fine," I told him. "I thought you guys were dead."

"We're fine. What's going on? They cancelled all flights, but no one is telling us anything."

I was shocked. "You don't know? Two planes crashed into the World Trade Center."

He was stunned. My mom immediately freaked out and was soon hysterical. I think her panic launched my father into Super Dad mode. He quickly took control, calming her and figuring out our next steps. We realized there was no chance we'd be flying back to Florida anytime soon, and the next thing I knew, we were in a rented minivan, headed south down the highway.

We drove nonstop, twenty-eight hours back home to Florida. Honestly, my focus the whole time was on the new boat I had waiting for me at home. Back then, my dad would give me a gift each time I came off tour, and for this one, it was a 23' Excalibur Volvo duo prop boat. It sounds strange now, considering I'd just witnessed 9/11 in person, but I was just an exhausted thirteen-year-old child star looking forward to a present from his dad and a good night's sleep in his own bed.

Chapter 2

Meet the Carters

It wasn't always like that—playing arenas, performing with Michael Jackson. Though honestly, for most of my life, it was pretty close. The time before fame, before our family was in the public eye, seems like a distant dream or someone else's memory. I was so young, being famous is really all I've ever known. It doesn't even seem that strange to me. That's my normal. The reality is, my older brother Nick was in the Backstreet Boys for as long as I can remember, and I became a childhood star not long after. Once all that hit, any semblance of a typical childhood was over for all of us.

Surrealness became my reality at an early age. I opened up for the Backstreet Boys in front of 50,000 fans in Germany when I was eight years old. At twelve, the *Aaron's Party* album was certified Triple Platinum. Traveling the world was my normal. As a preteen, I hung out with Beyoncé. Will and Jada Smith brought their kids to see me. Lindsay Lohan and Hilary Duff publicly fought over me. Hell, they made an action figure of me when I was thirteen. One Christmas was celebrated in Paris with Diana Ross, ice skating with her kids.

It all seemed normal. It took a long time for me to be able to look back and realize just how out of the ordinary my life was—I mean, all that craziness started before I lost my baby teeth.

But there *was* a time before all that, even if I don't remember it well. There aren't a lot of recollections from early childhood, at least a regular childhood like most people have. Some fond, if not fleeting, memories of riding dirt bikes when we lived in Tampa, running around the woods with my siblings, fishing with my dad, and going out on the boat with our family, but those are merely glimpses. Looking at an old family photo can trigger a memory from early childhood, but they are few and far between.

There is a good one from when I was pretty little. Growing up, Nick loved to play pranks on us. It was Christmastime, and we were still pretty poor back then without a lot of holiday decorations and presents, so Nick decided to entertain us. He tied up a bunch of tissues with hairbands to make them look like ghosts, then put them in front of a fan. When he turned the fan on, the tissues blew in the air, flying across the room like little ghosts.

Scared the crap out of me as a little boy. To this day, I still don't like fans in the dark because of that prank.

Stuff like that made me look up to him so much. Nick was my hero from about the time I could walk. He was eight years older than me, and aside from all the standard, cool big brother stuff, he also just happened to be in the biggest boy band in the world, doing exactly what I wanted to do. And he was happy to take me under his wing from early on.

Most people don't have any idea how much Nick loved rock music. Metal and grunge were his favorites growing up, which meant they were my favorites. He'd make me listen to Nirvana or Bush, and we'd sit in his room, singing along to CDs, imagining we were Kurt Cobain. I grew my hair real long, and we'd have headbanging contests. Even now, when I'm on stage, you'll see me whipping my head and headbanging as I perform. I got that from him. In those days, I wanted to be a rock star more than anything. Just like Nick.

I was his tag-along, his stunt double, a mini version of himself, and I think Nick was proud of that. He'd let me hang out with him and his friends, driving around in this badass forest green Chevy Silverado 1500 truck he'd bought with his Backstreet Boys money. We'd play paintball and go out on his boat. Just hang out as brothers, which I loved. He was a responsible and caring big brother, and I'm still appreciative of that. [*Talk about now.*]

I was the first actor in Nick's films. He'd put me in home videos of these action/adventure and murder mystery movies he created, big productions that he'd direct. He'd dress me up in period clothing or draw mustaches on me when the character called for it, calling out lines and direction. He had a real affinity for producing these movies, and I, of course, loved starring in them.

We had a blast just messing around in his room, singing Journey and stuff like MC Hammer and All For One. I was Nick's little protégé, and I loved it. I did a lot of singing and performing at home with all my siblings, but especially with him and my older sister, Leslie.

Leslie was probably the most talented out of all of us. She definitely had the biggest heart. The toughest too. She loved to sing and was really good at it from an early age. She and I used to perform The Carpenters' songs in the living room for our parents, especially around Christmastime. I guess, even then, we were trying to impress them, to show them we had what it took to be stars. When we'd have talent shows, Leslie would usually let me win because she knew it meant more to me. She was very caring and generous and a great big sister.

Ever since we were little, I always gravitated to Leslie. Whatever she told me to do, I'd do, no matter how crazy. For some reason, I always listened to her. Besides, I've always been a risk-taker. Always liked to do dangerous shit. Once, she convinced me to climb a tree with an umbrella. Then, she told me to jump and hold the umbrella open above my head to see if I could fly. I couldn't—and crashed to earth. She laughed and told me to try again. So, I did. Wouldn't you know it, I still couldn't fly. [*Did you get hurt?*]

Unfortunately, Leslie developed temperament problems and started to suffer from bipolar disorder at a young age, which made everything really hard for her. Combine that with the pressure of having both her older and younger brother find immediate success in entertainment, and she never really got the chance to flourish and take off as much as we had hoped. Her time was just cut too short.

Her passing from an overdose in 2012 was so sudden and such a shock to us all that we didn't know how to process it. I know I didn't. The family was already pretty estranged when she died, and I guess I had hoped the tragedy could bring the family closer. It didn't—instead, it created even more distance. More scarring, more sadness, as past pain that the family had tried to bury got reflected back at us after Leslie passed away.

I'm closest with my twin sister, Angel. She has a daughter now, my niece, and I'm so proud of the woman and mother she's become. She was destined to be a mom, and she's really good at it. Angel is so in love with Harper, and watching her interact with her daughter gives me such joy. [*Are you guys talking?*]

Angel was much more introverted than the rest of us growing up. She was more of a girly girl, more interested in her Barbie Dolls and cats than performing. Which was refreshing, since we had enough hams in the family.

Angel and I were close, as twins usually are. Maybe even closer than average twins. It always seemed like we knew what the other one was thinking, and we'd do everything together. Our parents really embraced the twin thing too and would dress us up alike. [*A memory of that?*]

But Angel was a lot more subdued than me. She was an overachiever in school and never went out of her way to get in trouble. Unlike some other people…

[*Need BJ story/background here.*]

There were some great times growing up in the Carter family, at least according to what boyhood recollections remain. But they didn't last long, and issues always seemed to pop up as we transitioned from an average American family to having every fight and slipup plastered across the tabloids.

Chapter 3

My Idol

Soon, Nick and the Backstreet Boys were an international sensation. What that meant for me was that my hero, my big brother, was no longer around. No more listening to The Gap Band and El DeBarge together, no more harmonizing to "No Diggity" by Blackstreet, no more playing basketball on the trampoline in our yard. It would be tour and appearance after tour and appearance for Nick (and soon for me too), starting at just the time I became a little boy and aware of everything going on around me. It was heartbreaking. I wanted to hang out with my big brother, and now he was gone all the time. I felt like I had suddenly lost my best friend.

I remember always asking my parents, "When will Nick be home? When will Nick be home?" and never getting a definite answer. Cell phones weren't as prevalent back then, so often, it was difficult to talk with him on the phone. As time went on, Nick's absences seemed longer and longer. We were still close, but there was no denying a drift.

Nick's success caused a lot of friction between my parents. I don't think my dad was as excited about everything that was going on, while Nick's success was the answer to all my mother's prayers. She wanted nothing more than to have rich and famous children. But while Nick was off fulfilling his dreams, those dreams took him away from the family. And it took my parents away from the rest of us. At least one of them would usually travel with him, and that spelled the end of any normal, nuclear family. I know, hard to believe, but we *were* normal once. Then, our parents began to fight—a lot—a theme that would only get worse over the years.

There were so many separations with the constant threat of divorce hanging over the family like a black cloud. My parents always brought us, the kids, into it. They'd sit us down in the living room and stand before us like it was an interrogation. We'd hear about their emotional problems and what the other one was doing wrong. Then, one by one, we were each told we had to pick who we wanted to live with. It was like picking a favorite with the other one right there.

Those ultimatums were a lot for us to take. As a young boy, I remember just how confused, how sad, I would be each time. I never knew what to do, whose side to take. They'd both blame each other, and I didn't know who to believe. Eventually, we'd all have to choose who we were going with.

I was a complete mama's boy, so I would always go with her. We'd grab the bare essentials and be off, usually staying at hotels or with friends. For some of the longer separations, she'd rent a house, sometimes taking us from Tampa to Orlando depending on where the business was at the time. They'd already pulled me from school by then, and I didn't pack much, so these exits were usually quick and without a lot of fanfare: big fight, family meeting, split up, hit the road. We all knew the moves were temporary, at least until the next one. They could last from weeks to months, but we'd always come back home.

As my career took off, I had so much pressure on me to sing and perform that the separations started to barely faze me anymore. Even that young, I was focused more on my career than anything else. Hotels and new rooms were already the norm for me, so I just went with the flow. I found it was better to stop paying attention to the drama than to focus on it, so that's what I did.

But I missed my sisters. Nick was usually gone by then, so he missed all the blowups, leaving only my sisters for support. And they would all go with our father, which was difficult on us. We were close, and during the times when I needed my sisters the most, we were apart. But I had always been scared of my dad; most people were scared of Bob Aaron. He was a former military police officer in the Army and very intimidating. He could be a scary dude, which is why I always chose my mom.

During all this, Nick's career continued excelling. I vaguely remember watching his progress throughout my early years, before the Backstreet Boys, how our mom had him in dancing and singing lessons. He was always auditioning for commercials or boy bands. It didn't seem out of the ordinary to me that Nick regularly got to leave school for performances and contests. Besides, the routine worked. Before long, he started to get gigs and become better known.

There was his performance on Star Search, singing Frank Sinatra. Then, he started performing at Tampa Bay Buccaneers football games. He got a few commercials and was even in the background of *Edward Scissorhands*. But it was one of those auditions in Orlando in 1993 that changed everything for the Carter family.

I was five at the time, so Nick making the band is kind of a blur for me. I just remember when this big, gregarious guy I thought of like Santa Claus selected Nick for the boy band he was putting together, it was a huge deal in our family. That guy was Lou Pearlman, and the band was the Backstreet Boys. Once that happened, our family would never be the same, even if we didn't realize it at the time.

I didn't really know what to make of it all, but nothing seemed exceptional or out of place to me or my siblings. We'd all watched Nick build to this point, and it just seemed normal that he was becoming a star. He'd always been a ham and a performer—that's what we knew him as. His success seemed like a natural progression that everyone was just cool with. It was just like, okay, my big brother is in this huge boy band, making a ton of money and touring all over the world. Cool but not unexpected. I can tell you this: Being around it all made me want to do it.

There were perks to having your brother in the Backstreet Boys. I would go to all their rehearsals, all the recording sessions in Orlando. Just this precocious little blond seven-year-old, running around these cool multi-million-dollar studios, never once considering that I didn't belong there. It's like the son of a baseball player hanging around the locker room. That culture and atmosphere just seem like second nature. I didn't think it was anything special to see R. Kelly coming in and out of the studio, or [*who else*].

[*Talk about your relationship with the other band members.*]

I got to start missing a lot of school to hang out with Nick and the band. A lot of times, my parents weren't even there; it was just me and Nick. I think they thought they could control me better knowing I was with him. At least they knew when I'd be home. Honestly, I don't know why they let me do it, but so many times, it would be just Nick and I, driving to the studio together instead of going to school.

There were always pool tables in these places, and I'd end up hanging out in the community area with the adults, shooting pool while inadvertently soaking up information about the music industry. [*What would they say? What did they think of you?*] I'd watch each guy go into the booth and cut their vocals… [*Like what? Any drugs or anything?*]

Then, there were the shows, being backstage with the band. I didn't go on tour with them back then, but I remember the first show they did in Orlando. All the screaming girls, the speakers the size of my house. [*More.*]

When Nick would get off the road, he'd come home with garbage bags full of stuffed animals that fans had given him, and he'd give them to us. There was always so much free stuff. Lou Pearlman had a massive room at Trans Continental Records stocked full of all the gifts fans had sent to the band. Jewelry, trinkets, toys, [*what else*], and me and my sisters would get to go and raid this room, take anything we wanted. It was great.

I loved all the free stuff, and I'd be incredibly excited to see what he brought me but also a little discouraged because I wanted to earn my own stuff. Some of the teddy bears would even have Nick's name on them, a glaring reminder that they weren't meant for me. Those teddy bears were the first things to inspire me to become a musician; I didn't want a handout—I wanted my name on teddy bears.

As the Backstreet Boys continued to take off, the money started rolling in, and my parents started spending it.

First, they did a bunch of updates to the house. A new kitchen, updated bathrooms, fresh flooring, that type of stuff. We splurged on new toys: boats, jet skis, dirt bikes. Clothes and shoes. Fancier meals. We became more materialistic as a family, just spending and spending.

Eventually, we acquired so much stuff that we ran out of room. We were going to need a bigger house.

It was our mom who pushed the move to California from Florida. I don't think anyone else wanted to go out there. But it was the home of the rich and the famous—and the entertainment industry. She already had ideas about replicating Nick's fame with me and figured that goal would be easier to achieve near LA.

Before we moved, she and I flew out and stayed in Venice while we researched where to live. [*Talk about going to Venice and house hunting with your mom.*]

Nick, who was responsible for our sudden influx of money, didn't even come with us to Cali. He had his own house in Florida by that point and stayed there. For the rest of us, it was a mansion on the bluffs of Palos Verdes, California, the Pacific Ocean a steely blue backdrop for our new lifestyle. Again, funded by Nick.

Nick spoiled the family back then, there's no way around it. And I don't think that any of us truly appreciated it at the time. We just looked around and saw all this cash he was making and sharing with us, and we probably felt a little entitled. I think the whole family felt like we had a right to his money, like we deserved it. In some senses, Nick became a prisoner to the money. He felt responsible for us and was taking care of a lot of people, though he was only a teenager. When he turned eighteen and had sole possession of his money, he put his foot down and became more protective of what he was spending, but in the beginning, I think our parents treated it like having a blank check. But once he could legally possess the money he was earning, the houses, cars, and toys that he had been buying for the rest of us kind of went away. Which meant that my parents needed a new gravy train.

Our household was obsessed with the entertainment industry and ensuring that one of us would be the next to hit it big. My parents—especially my mother—became laser focused on their other children also becoming stars. My dad had come around a little and was proud of what Nick was doing, but as Nick's career (and mine) took off, it changed the father/son dynamic. To most men, it's important to be the family provider. In our household, that role changed early on, and I don't think that ever sat right with my father. He thought of himself as the protector, the provider, but his sons ended up earning the money that kept the family afloat. I don't know that he ever got over that before he died. [*What would you tell him now?*]

The race to be the next Carter child star was on. They tried us all out; it became like the lottery—who was going to be the next to hit it big? We all envied what Nick was doing, but it soon became clear that I was the only one seriously interested in pursuing music from an early age. I watched what Nick was doing and wanted to be exactly like him. I got the bug—bad. I wanted to be a star too.

    I was all of seven years old.

Chapter 4
I Got the Bug

When I was in the third grade, my school held a talent show. I think Nick was already in BSB at the time, but this was before they really blew up. My parents told me to enter the competition, so I did. Hell, my brother was in the Backstreet Boys. I was going to win that damn competition.

I remember that I was wearing a new pair of red Jordans. The school had given them to me, charity I guess, because I'd had the same pair of shoes for so long. This was before Nick's money started rolling in. Our family was considered poor, not that we kids really noticed or cared. My adolescent mind was just amped to go out and win this talent show in front of everybody in my new red Jordans.

It was hot on the stage in Ruskin Elementary's cafeteria. The bright lights, super white and blinding, took me by surprise when I walked out. But right away, it felt good being up there in front of all those people. This was where I wanted to be. Where I was meant to be. All those showcases with my brother and sisters in our living room, all the daydreaming of being a rock star. This was where it had led me.

I remember how nervous I was, my palms sweating. [*Do you get nervous today? How did those nerves compare to how you are today before a show?*] But I don't think the nerves were about performing; they were about having something to prove. I *needed* to beat those other people. To feel like a superstar, a hero. As I watched the other kids go on before me, I gave myself no option except winning this competition.

I knew my parents and sisters were somewhere in the audience, and I wanted to impress them. Angel was competing as well, probably against her wishes, singing Britney Spears. Nick couldn't make it—he was on the road—but that was okay. I'd win this thing and show everyone I was just as good as he was.

I walked on stage, heart pumping, and rocked out to Tom Petty's "Running Down A Dream." I knew I'd killed it. After the performance, I soaked in the applause, then exited stage left and waited until my classmates finished performing so I could collect my trophy. I think it ended up being a little medal, but whatever. I waited through "Over the Rainbow" rendition after "Ice Ice

Baby" after, I don't know, some Irish jigs and probably kids moonwalking to "Thriller." Didn't matter—I was better than them all. But then there was this one girl who sang Selena's "Como La Flor." I had to admit, she was pretty good. I had a funny feeling after she got off the stage but still figured I had this thing in the bag. I expected to win.

When they read my name as the runner-up, I couldn't believe what I was hearing. The Selena wannabe had beaten me! It took a good deal of effort and self-control to not get visibly upset, not to have an outburst. Thankfully, I didn't act like a sore loser, though I certainly wanted to. Still do. Can't believe that bitch beat me. Joking, of course. I'm over it by now. Kinda.

[*Writer's note: I once texted Aaron to see if he remembered the name of the little girl who won. His response: "Nope lol She'd be dead. lol"*]

It was a quiet car ride home. Angel had not done well and was even more upset than I was. [*Did she hate performing?*] I remember thinking to myself what a mistake it had been to have gotten my hopes up in the first place. I was the youngest in my family; I never expected to win at anything, ever. At home, if I beat Nick in a video game, he'd get so pissed that I didn't even want to win anymore. It wasn't worth his wrath. So, I wouldn't try. But that reluctance to beat him led to the opposite mindset outside the house. I wanted to beat *everyone* at *everything*. And in our family, that generally meant performing. And I had just failed at that.

But to my surprise, my parents seemed thrilled with what I had done at the talent show. They lit up when talking about my performance and implored me to do more. In fact, that was when they started me in singing and dancing lessons. This was the beginning of my stage life.

It was also about the time that the fighting between them started to get bad. Or at least when I began to notice it. There had always been arguments, and maybe I was too young for their severity to register, but as the money and fame increased, the fights' frequency and ferocity seemed to pick up accordingly.

Alcohol certainly fueled their battles. As kids, we didn't realize how much drinking our parents were doing. But it was a lot, and it led to some huge fights.

Once, Angel and I were jumping on the trampoline in the backyard. Our parents were inside fighting, but we just ignored them, having fun playing by ourselves. Suddenly, we heard what sounded like a gunshot. We stopped jumping and looked around, unsure of what had happened. Nothing seemed out of the ordinary. The backyard was quiet, the sun still shining, birds chirping. The sound didn't come again, and nothing appeared disturbed. We shrugged and started jumping again.

We'd later learn that my mother had been wasted and had taken out a gun and told my father she was going to blow his head off. When she aimed it at his face, he'd smacked her arm away and the gun had gone off, shooting out the window, past us on the trampoline, and lodging in our neighbor's house. No one realized how close she had come to killing her own children.

While all this turmoil was going on, my parents decided that this would be the perfect time to immerse me into the world of music. After all, the only thing better than having one money-making child star is having two. Despite my failure at the talent show, the performance had buoyed their hopes for me, and they went full speed ahead with my musical instruction. My parents had seen the formula work with Nick, and it was time to replicate it. Soon, my brother would be eighteen with full control of his money. Someone had to pay the family bills. It was determined I had the best chance of doing that.

So, at eight years old, Bob and Jane took me out of public school, and I began to attend Paragon Music School in Tampa. But in reality, I became a full-time musician. I had been dabbling since six or seven, but now, it was serious. Grind time. Suddenly, instead of math class, I found myself taking guitar lessons. Instead of recess, it was rehearsals. Vocal coaches instead of guidance counselors.

My career officially began with the creation of a rock band called Dead End, put together by the music school I attended. It was made up of me, a few classmates, and this like sixty- or seventy-year-old teacher who played the piano. I was the lead singer, and we'd perform in coffee shops and other small venues around Tampa. It was how they got me used to performing regularly and being in a band.

Soon, I had the attention of the Backstreet Boys' management, and it was my turn for Lou Pearlman to "discover" me. Since Lou was managing the Backstreet Boys, he was always around our family back then. We all adored him. He was this big, lovable guy whom we all respected so much.

Of course, he would later go to prison for defrauding investors of hundreds of millions of dollars, and we'd learn he stole massive amounts from me and my family, but at that time, we thought he walked on water. Everything he touched seemed to turn to gold. So, when Lou and Johnny Wright—who'd also managed New Kids on the Block, Britney Spears, the Jonas Brothers, etc.— said they wanted me to record a song, I couldn't believe it. This was my chance to show the world and my family that I had what it took.

Lou and Johnny had essentially created the Backstreet Boys and NSYNC and were the titans of pop at the time. Talk about having a formula—they had a tried-and-true one and decided I would be the next one they'd apply it to. I don't know that they had high expectations, but the risks were low. Johnny told my mom, "Hey, let's have Aaron come in and record a song and see what happens." So, we did, almost as a joke.

They took me to Lou's studio in Orlando to record a cover of the Jets' "Crush on You." I think I was eight years old. It took me five days to record that one song. It was nerve-racking having all these adults—the musicians, managers, producers, engineers—watching me, trying to get me to sing this song properly. I was a little kid and had no idea what I was doing. I was still learning how to sing and too young to take instruction well. Gary Carolla, a producer who worked with the Backstreet Boys and NSYNC, sang along with me and ended up unintentionally overdubbing the whole song. If you listen to the studio-released version of my "Crush on You" cover, you can hear his voice over mine.

The song became a massive hit overnight, and we were off to the races. The younger siblings of all of Nick's fans suddenly became Aaron Carter fans, just like that. They had me do a music video for the song, and then I was opening for the Backstreet Boys in Germany. Before I knew it, I had a record deal and was recording a full album. The whirlwind had officially begun.

Chapter 5
A Star Is Born

My parents were thrilled with their youngest son's success, as were Lou and Johnny. My mom had all these ideas about my image. The blond hair, the bowl cut, professional photographs. She'd dress me up in these orange overalls that I guess became my signature, but I thought I looked like a fucking Crush soda can. The money started rolling in (I assume), and everyone was getting rich, though I was too young for the money I was producing to be in my name. No longer was school a consideration; the only focus became keeping the Aaron Carter machine in full swing.

I wasn't privy to exactly what my parents and management team had in store for me next, but as soon as that first single took off, so did their plans. They wasted no time in putting the machine in overdrive. I started doing every interview under the sun, training around the clock, booking concerts all over the world, traveling nonstop for all of it with no rest and no breaks. I was just a kid—who was I to argue with Lou or my parents about my schedule? I did what I was told.

[*What was next immediately? Did they present a plan?*]

I remember it being very surreal every time we went to Lou Pearlman's office in Orlando. It was in the penthouse of this beautiful building, decorated immaculately with blimps and gold records and awards and trophies and Star Wars figurines and old-school Frank Sinatra dolls. It had a great Rat Pack vibe mixed with this rich, elegant Jewish taste. It could have been intimidating, and for some, it probably was, but to me, Lou was so friendly and warm, I felt like I was just hanging out with a really rich older friend. A friend who could make my career. To me, Lou was like a real-life Santa Claus—this jolly guy who was offering me and our family so much.

[*Ever go to the blimp hangar where bands would rehearse?*]

We'd sit in his office, and he'd tell me, "You ready to do this? You're going to be great. I know you got it in you." And I'd just sit there with my parents while he'd stare at me and compliment me. [*Creepy? Was there ever anything inappropriate?*] Honestly, I barely paid attention to Lou when he was going over the plans for my career. My attention was more focused on the way my dad would look at me during Lou's pep talks. He'd get this intense what I like to imagine was a proud look on his face, like, "Yeah, my son's a badass." It felt great knowing my dad thought highly of me. It made me want to do more, to do better.

So, I did what I was told. I was nine when I recorded *Aaron Carter*. The self-titled album was basically a litmus test to see if I had what it took, and it ended up being a resounding success. It sold over a million copies worldwide, and I toured the globe in 1998, singing "Crush on You," "Crazy Little Party Girl," and "I'm Gonna Miss You Forever" to sold-out shows.

People often ask me when I realized I was famous. What was my "aha" moment? And it's funny because I never had that eureka moment, even after the instant success of that first song. Yeah, I was really young when it all happened, so my total consciousness wasn't even fully developed yet, but screaming fans and girls flocking to us had always been a part of my life because of Nick. To me, all that was normal. If anything, the accolades seemed to be part of a competition. A popularity contest. I was back to competing against Nick, entering talent shows. How many fans could I get? How much love and adoration could I receive? How many people could I impress? That's why I did it.

I guess the real differentiator, when I became proud of what I was accomplishing, was when fans showed up at the gates to our house—not to get a glimpse of Nick but to see me. They were Aaron Carter fans. I loved the adoration. I lived for it. And I've been chasing it ever since.

Chapter 6
Neverland

I only went to Neverland once, and I ended up spending the night, sleeping on a cot in Michael Jackson's bedroom, just feet from his own bed.

It was 2003, and Michael was throwing a huge birthday bash for himself at his Neverland Ranch. Everyone from _____ to _____ was invited. [*Performers? What else was part of the party?*] Michael asked Nick and I to attend. [*How did you both feel about the invite?*] I was fifteen at the time, living in Florida with my parents and sisters. [*Did you fly in special for the party? Was Nick based in LA or FL?*]

Neverland Ranch, of course, was Michael's famous compound in Santa Barbara County. A few years earlier, my family had actually lived on the other side of the mountain from Neverland in Santa Ynez, though we had never visited Michael's ranch. We always knew he lived nearby, but it wasn't until moving 3,000 miles away that I was seeing Neverland for the first time.

I was still bitter about moving from there when I was thirteen. The relocation back to Florida had been for my parents to realize a champagne wish of theirs: to live in the Keys. Now that we were able to afford their dream, they had uprooted the family and transplanted us once again. I was pissed and let them know it, but no one gave me a say in the matter. Even though I likely paid for our new lodgings in Florida without realizing it.

The home we moved to ended up being more like a compound with several different houses on the property and each kid living on their own. [*Did that seem cool to you? You had your own home?*] The episode of *MTV Cribs* I did shows a good bit of the property and some of our toys, though I was in a bit of a daze while we were filming. You see, about ten minutes before we started, I found out that my parents' divorce had been finalized. I was told that after filming wrapped on the *Cribs* episode, I had to pack up all my stuff and move.

But I had never wanted to leave California in the first place. For once in my life, I'd felt comfortable somewhere. I had absolutely loved the ranch we'd lived on in the sprawling hills of Santa Ynez. It had felt like home, a rare and cherished sentiment during a stunted childhood spent mostly in hotels.

I remember being able to just do normal boy shit when we lived there. Shooting rattlesnakes with my shotgun, riding dirt bikes, doing target practice with a bow and arrow, running around with my dogs. Being a kid. But it was short lived—three years—and with how much touring I was doing, I was rarely home to enjoy those things anyway. Now, I was excited to go back.

Michael sent a limo to our hotel to pick up Nick and I and bring us to Neverland for his birthday. I remember on the drive up how familiar everything felt. The contours of the road, the street signs, even the smell of the air. If there was any place that I'd lived where I felt like I belonged, it was Santa Ynez. I missed it then and still do to this day.

When we arrived at the party, there were already thousands of people milling about. It was a who's who. [*Who was there? Describe the scene. What did you do before the cake cutting?*]

When it was time to cut the cake, Michael brought Nick and I (among others) up on stage with him. I was just a punk kid and didn't care how famous anyone was, so I decided to smash the cake in Michael's face on stage. Somewhere, there is video of that. [*Did everyone sing happy birthday? What was the atmosphere up there before smashing it?*]

JoJo Wright, the famous disc jockey on KIIS-FM in Los Angeles, was on the stage with us that night. He still loves to tell the story about the cake. He was close with Michael as well, and that fun-loving display—Michael not only didn't get upset about us hitting him with the cake, he encouraged it—was a great example of how Michael was just a kind, goofy kid at heart. In fact, in between giggles, and with his face covered in cake, he threw and smeared what was left of it on Nick and I, and it devolved into a fun food fight in front of all the partygoers.

[*What did you do after the cake?*]

The party started to break up, and a golf cart showed up to take a few of us to the main house. My brother; Michael's right-hand man, Raffles; Rodney Jerkins, who was a producer on Michael's *Invincible* album; some other bald dude named Peter (I think); me; and Michael all jumped in the [*describe the*] cart and headed [*how far/direction?*] to the house.

When we arrived, the actor Chris Tucker joined us, and we all took seats around this huge couch in [*what type of room?*]. It was my first (and only) time seeing Michael's house. I took a minute to look around and take everything in. The ornateness of the house astounded me. It was immaculate. Statues all over the place, ancient carpets, gold helmets and spoons and stuff just stacked everywhere, not even organized. I couldn't even tell you what half the stuff was. The place looked like somewhere an Egyptian pharaoh would live. That was probably the only time that I felt starstruck by Michael Jackson. When you just consider how much money all that cost, yeah, I was impressed.

We sat around, really not doing much. [*Talking? Joking? What?*] Then, Raffles said to Michael, "Hey, Michael, don't you have something for Aaron?"

Michael looked up, suddenly remembering something. He smiled coyly, then stood and walked to a closet.

"That's right, I do," he said, pulling out the jacket that he had worn at the MSG concert the night before September 11th. He handed it to me.

"Treat this well, Apple Head," he told me. [*When/why did he start calling you that?*] He started to go into some speech about how I needed to keep working hard and follow in his footsteps, but honestly, I wasn't even listening. I didn't care what he was saying. I just wanted the jacket. And now I had it. I told you, I was a shithead back then.

[*Did you put it on? What did the other people say? Atmosphere?*]

After a while, Nick got up and said that he was ready to leave. It was probably around midnight, and the party was pretty much over. But I wasn't ready to go. I was hanging out with my idol right next to my boyhood home. There was no way I was calling it a night. I relayed that to Nick as spoiled younger siblings do to big brothers, and he responded in kind. Namely, he didn't want to hear it. He didn't want to be there anymore and wasn't going to be convinced to stay by me or anyone else. Nick and I had a short conversation, and at the end of it, he left.

I called my mom to tell her I was staying. She wasn't happy, but I told her that it was fine, that Michael would get me back to the hotel she was staying at the next day. I explained how much fun I was having hanging out and how nice Michael was. Finally, she relented, telling me to check in and that she'd see me tomorrow.

By that point, it was starting to clear out. Only me, Chris, and Michael were left. Earlier, I had seen Michael's security team patrolling the property on four-wheelers. I knew exactly what I wanted to do next.

"Let's go four-wheeling," I said, more a demand than a suggestion. I used to live in these mountains; I knew them well and was fiending to get back out there. Michael didn't seem terribly excited by the prospect, but he also seemed eager to please, so he took out the walkie-talkie he carried to communicate with the Neverland staff and told whomever he needed to that we wanted some four-wheelers.

We walked outside, and already the four-wheelers were waiting, engines idling. Cool. Michael, Chris, and I got our gear on and boom, we were off. We started riding around the grounds, shooting up and down the mountain. Having a blast, shrieking and joking and laughing, but the whole time, I couldn't help but think about my old house on the other side of the mountain. All the memories came rushing back again. The smell of the desert, the trees, the flowers, the angle of the stars and the way the moon shone down, the color of the brush, the dirt—everything was so familiar to me.

It was an incredibly surreal experience. I was doing my favorite thing in the whole world with one of my favorite people whom I looked up to so much. Not that it really registered at the time. It took years to be able to reflect and recognize the remarkability of that experience. But back then, I was just a kid having a rare moment of freedom on a high-powered motorized vehicle.

We rode for hours. Up and down, [*where? What did you see? Did you see your old house?*] At some point, I began to lead the way. Michael was driving like an old lady, and it was getting annoying. Both Chris and I wanted to go fast and kept yelling back to him, "Come on, man, speed up a little bit!" [*Were you making fun of him?*] Mind you, this was at nighttime, so it wasn't the safest activity we could have been participating in. But to his credit, Michael started driving faster, trying to keep up as I navigated us through the brush and trees [*cactus? What else up there?*] with only [*describe the headlight glow*].

At one point, we turned a sharp corner, revealing a sudden ledge directly in our path that led over the side of the mountain. I skidded to a stop while Chris pulled around me sharply, almost going off the hill. Then, Michael's ass came flying around the corner. Him and his ATV went right over the ledge, plummeting off the side of the mountain. Chris and I just stood there, mouths open, not believing what we were seeing: Michael Jackson airborne on an ATV, screaming the whole way down.

I remember exactly what I was thinking as I watched the four-wheeler tumble down the mountain, its headlights bouncing all over the place: *Fuck. I just killed Michael Jackson.*

Chris and I ran down to see if he was alright. His machine was stuck in a ravine, and Michael was trying to pull it out. [*What did he say?*] I was shocked and recall my next thoughts as well: *How is this motherfucker still alive?*

But he seemed fine for the most part with only sticks and leaves poking out of his helmet and some cuts on his hands. We were able to free the ATV and get it back up the hill. Our ATVing adventure was over for the night. We headed back to the house, where Chris said he was going to crash in a guesthouse he referred to as the "movie theater house." I guess that's where he always stayed.

Michael and I went into the main house alone and headed to his bedroom area. There were these French doors that opened onto a patio, and we hung out there just talking. It was probably three or four in the morning. He told me about his life. I told him about mine. [*What else did you talk about? Anything strike you about the conversation?*]

At some point, he asked me if I drank. [*What did he offer?*] I told him no, I didn't, but that I smoked weed and asked if he had any. He said he didn't but that he would get me some for tomorrow. "Cool," I said, and we kept talking about how similar our lives were.

His whole demeanor towards me was nurturing and caring. He kept asking questions about my life: Was I working too hard? Did I like what I was doing? Did I feel too much pressure? I felt that he was genuinely interested in me and concerned for my wellbeing. He knew what it was like to be a child star and get taken advantage of. He didn't want it to happen to me.

After a while, I said I was ready for bed. I hadn't really thought about where I would sleep; obviously, there were tons of rooms in the house. But he pulled out this cot next to his bed that was already made. I never asked for the cot, but there it was. I didn't care. I was tired. He turned out the lights and got in his bed, and we went to sleep.

A couple of hours later, something woke me. I sat up and found Michael at the foot of my cot in his tighty-whitey underwear. [*Was he touching you or anything? Standing? Laying down?*] I don't know if he was sleepwalking or what, but he seemed to still be asleep. [*Describe his face.*]

"What the fuck!?" I shouted and shook him a little to wake him. "Go back to your bed!"

He looked startled, like he was surprised to be there. He just mumbled, "Okay," then got back into his bed, and we both went back to sleep. I never asked him about it, and we never mentioned it. When I woke up in the morning, he was gone from the room.

I thought it strange to find myself alone in his bedroom. I got up and started walking around the house, trying to find Michael. Everything looked different in the daytime, and I had no idea where the hell I was going. Not to mention, the place was huge. Staff scuttled about everywhere and didn't seem especially surprised to find a kid wandering around. No one tried to help me, barely even looking at me. They all knew I was there but wouldn't acknowledge me. I figured someone would be like, "Hey, kid, why are you wandering around? Can I help you?" I kept asking people if they knew where Michael was, but it was almost like they were ignoring me. Mum was the word around there.

Eventually, I got pissed. I had found my way outside and loudly announced something along the lines of, "Excuse me, can someone tell me where the fuck Michael is because I'm done wandering around here!" I was a little shit. I didn't give a fuck. That did the trick, and someone directed me to his office, where I discovered him opening birthday gifts.

"Oh, hey. What's up, Apple Head?" he said when I walked in. "Check out what Michael Jordan sent me." He pointed to a sculpture in the corner. It was of Michael Jordan in his original white and red 23 jersey.

Honestly, I didn't really care. I was like, "Dude, your birthday was yesterday. Where's my weed?" That was all I cared about. I was fifteen and smoked a lot of weed. Still do.

"Oh yeah, I got it," he said, all proud, and pulled out a manila bubble-wrapped envelope. We headed to his studio and hung out there, listening to music. [*What music?*] He showed me the weed there. When I saw how high quality it was, I got really excited. It was me, Michael, and this six-foot-six blond assistant guy who lived on the ranch and who I knew had a big dirt bike. I just wanted to smoke and ride this dude's bike.

"Where should we smoke?" Michael asked.

"I have the perfect idea," I said. "I have my learner's permit. Let's take the Bentley and pretend we're going to get pizza. We can drive over to my old property and smoke there. I know the safe places. I used to smoke weed there all the time." I'd started smoking weed when I was about eleven; I was a pro at finding places to do so.

He agreed, and we went inside so he could get some money for the pizza. [*Describe the safe.*] He opened a safe, and when he closed it, the stack of cash in his hand must have been at least twenty grand.

"Dude, we don't need that. It's like twenty bucks for pizza," I said. It struck me that he had no idea how much pizza cost. [*What did he say/do?*] We grabbed the weed and some blunts and got in the Bentley. I drove with

Michael in the passenger seat while this tall ass assistant sat in the back.

We drove for a few miles before I turned down a little dirt road lined with grapevines. It had been years since I'd lived there, but somehow, I still recognized the turnoff. The windy path was shaded with [*describe the road*]. It looked like the Greek countryside, just remote and dusty and beautiful and familiar.

The road led us to a spot overlooking Heaven's Gate, the hundred-acre property my family had owned until selling when I was thirteen. I looked over the familiar landscape. When my family had lived there, we had turned the acres of vineyard into a four-wheeling haven, riding ATVs and dirt bikes up and down the mountain for hours. I could see my old house from where we parked, and I realized just how much I missed that place. Showing Michael my old home while rolling a blunt in his Bentley was quite nostalgic for me. [*Did he have any commentary on you guys living so close together?*]

"Check this out," Michael said and hit play on the car's stereo. It was his new album, *Invincible*. I don't even think it was out yet. [*Was it a CD? What was his demeanor? Did he sing along? Proud? Embarrassed? What did you think about the music your first time hearing it?*]

We started hotboxing the Bentley, and Michael was hitting the blunt like a G. He knew what he was doing—Michael smoked like a thug. Me, I was my normal fifteen-year-old cool guy self, blowing smoke rings and French inhaling like the badass I envisioned myself to be back then.

The weed was good. We kept smoking, talking about [*what*], and listening to Michael's music. As we got higher and I watched Michael, I started tripping out a little bit. He had obviously had a lot of plastic surgery, and it looked [*like what*]. Just being stoned and looking at his face kind of tripped me out. He kept popping and locking his head with the music, the movements so perfect and robotic that *that* started to creep me out. Enough so that I had to get out of the car at one point to take a timeout. I walked to the back of the vehicle to collect my thoughts. I mean, I was high, he was high, we were listening to his music, my old house was right there. It all was pretty nuts and overwhelming. After I took a moment, I got back in the car and acted like everything was fine.

We took a long, windy road back to Michael's house with him driving. On the way, I noticed these mini horses on the side of the road that we'd always see when we lived there, and I started to get a little sad. I was happy that they were still there but sad because I realized I may never be back there to see them again. [*More.*] We stopped in this little Danish town called Solvang for the pizza [*who got out to get it?*] and then headed back to Neverland.

Meanwhile, back at the ranch, I was stoned and full of pizza and just wanted to cruise around on one of the dirt bikes I had seen. But Michael insisted on showing me the property, and we started walking around while he [*bragged about everything?*]

"You like crocodiles?" he asked.

Huh? "Sure..." I answered, wondering why the hell he asked me that.

He got this glimmer in his eye and a tight little smirk on his face and pushed his hair behind his ear. "Come on, Apple Head, I got something to show you."

[*Describe it.*] This fucker next jumped in the crocodile pit and grabbed the tail of some huge crocodile and started swinging it around. I don't know if they were trained or if he always did that shit, but I was like, "Oh shit, he's gonna die again."

At this point, honestly, I'd had enough of Michael. I couldn't be around him anymore. Keep in mind, I was fifteen years old, and this guy was an adult to me. I'd just spent the better part of two days with him.

Don't get me wrong, we had a great time. He's super fun to be around. Sweet and genuine and just a great guy.

Hanging out with him like that was a dream the whole twenty-four hours. One of the coolest stories I have. I never really thought twice about the bed incident and certainly never held it against him. I truly believe he was asleep when it happened, maybe on a sedative or something (I didn't see anything like that, but he could have taken something or been administered something when I was in a different room), and did not know what he was doing. For years, I cherished the story of that day and only told it to the people I was closest with.

But come on. He was messing with a crocodile, and in case I haven't stressed it enough, I really like smoking weed and riding dirt bikes. I can be alone with my thoughts when riding. I feel free and can clear my head. I actually sing. [*Sing what?*] And that day, I just wanted to get on one of those damn dirt bikes and ride around the Neverland grounds for hours by myself. Finally, that's what I did.

When I returned, a limo was waiting for me. It was time to go home. Michael and I said our quick goodbyes: "Thanks for coming. Hope you had fun." "Yeah, man, let's do it again." Then, I hopped into the limo and left Neverland.

The car took me to my mother's hotel, the Sheraton Universal in Burbank. I went up to the room, exhausted but content, only to be greeted by my mom with two detectives. They started peppering me with questions, wanting to know if anything had happened with me and Michael. They asked me over and over, essentially trying to get me to say he did something sexual. He hadn't, so I didn't say shit. I was used to handling cops at fifteen, and I wasn't telling them shit. Not about the weed, not about him getting up in the middle of the night. I basically ignored them altogether—all I heard was noise, and I just gave them attitude and told everyone to fuck off.

The whole situation really made me pissed at my mom. I had no idea what her intention was. Why would she call detectives to come question me? Was she trying to extort Michael? I had no idea. I love my mom, but that was the type of thing that she would do, and I didn't want to be a part of it. So, I didn't say shit, and the cops finally left. [*You guys fly back to FL right away?*]

Michael and I stayed in touch for years, often talking on the phone. [*What was your relationship when he died?*] I always loved Michael and had a lot of respect for him. He was a very loving human being who experienced a lot of fake love in his life, as I have. We stayed in touch over the phone for years, and eventually, he just stopped calling. [*I am unsure whether Aaron meant "he—Aaron—stopped calling" or "he—Michael—stopped calling."*]

Writer's note: Those six chapters represent the sum of the work Aaron and I "finished." We reviewed those chapters in detail, editing, updating, and ensuring they were complete and accurate. However, as you can see, I did have some clarifying questions I did not have a chance to ask and left those inline.

What follows is my best attempt at transcribing the pages upon pages of notes from our interviews—again, some done in person; others, over the phone. Aaron's words are edited as little as possible to keep true to his meaning, even if in some places that meaning is not clear.

In many areas, he contradicts himself; I found that wasn't uncommon with Aaron, but because there is no opportunity to clarify, those contradictions are included as he relayed them to me. Where appropriate, I have included explanations as best I could to interpret Aaron's comments from, in some cases, over three years ago.

For the most part, you can consider these direct quotes from Aaron. I hope it gives you some insight into the mind of a tortured soul.

ON HIS RELATIONSHIP WITH MICHAEL JACKSON

Michael Jackson became aware of who I was at a young age. I was following in his footsteps. I was seven when I became a household name; he was seven or eight when it happened for him. He understood what I was going through.

Gary Carolla produced my first album that broke Michael Jackson's record for the most singles. That's how Michael heard about me. He would send messages about me to my team, telling them to "take care of Aaron," and saying that I was a good performer.

In 2001, my parents, who were my managers at the time, got a call that Michael Jackson wanted me to be on a charity song for him. I'd been dying to meet Michael Jackson, but we'd never crossed paths before. I was excited to meet him and record with him, but it wasn't that out of the ordinary for me to be around famous people. I was used to that life, especially with Nick being in the Backstreet Boys. They had sold twenty-five to thirty million records at that point.

Me, my mom, and Nick flew into LA from the Florida Keys where we were living at the time. Me and Nick did the song for Michael Jackson, and Michael told me he was impressed with me and my soul.

I wasn't nervous recording the song, but I did look up to him. After doing the song, I signed the inside of a Bentley that he owned and then auctioned off for charity. That was the first time we met in person, and after, I thanked him for having me and told him, "See you later." Michael gave me his cell phone number and would call to check in on me quite often. He was always worried about me. He called me Apple Head. I always got cool big brother vibes from Michael.

After recording that song, when I got back home, he called me and asked if I wanted to open up for the Jackson 5's twentieth anniversary tribute at Madison Square Garden.

I never told that story about waking up with Michael next to me in his underwear in his room because I didn't know how it would affect his kid. Besides, it didn't trip me out too much. I really think he was just sleepwalking; I don't think he had any bad intentions. He was like me, a stunted kid stuck in a man's body. I held that story near and dear.

ON GETTING HIS START IN MUSIC

My first single, "Crush on You," was recorded as a joke. Lou Pearlman and Johnny Wright, the guys who created me, had Gary Carolla produce that song. I barely remember recording it and don't even remember where we did it at. But it was a huge hit, which I think was a pleasant surprise to the adults who put me up to it (my parents, the producers, management, etc.) But once that happened, it was on. My mom was hellbent on making me a star.

♡

ON HIS CRAZY SCHEDULE AS A CHILD

Back then is kind of hard to remember, but they took me out of school almost every day. Soon, I stopped going altogether, and they got me the same tutor as Nick had, who travelled with me. Instead of being with my friends in school, I was touring, recording, doing interviews with the press, and taking music lessons. But all I really wanted to do was sleep and spend time with my family. It was all very monotonous, almost like *Groundhog Day*. That's what happens when you do the same thing every single day. A nine-year-old shouldn't have that type of schedule.

I never was allowed to get enough sleep as a kid. I remember one time when I was nine, I didn't want to perform, and I hit my mom with a hair dryer. I didn't wanna work. I remember locking myself in the bathroom of one of our hotel rooms and falling asleep in the bathtub because I needed more sleep. My mom broke down the door, afraid I was drowning in there.

[*Writer's note: This is very chilling to recount given what we now know about how he died.*]

I would sleep wherever I could while touring: laying on speakers, luggage carts, on airplanes and buses, curled up in a ball, just hoping everyone would leave me alone and I could rest. I never could.

I remember touring in Germany right after "Crush on You" when I was opening for the Backstreet Boys. It was cold and rainy, and we had a show early in the day. I wanted to sleep in, but my mom wouldn't let me. She was always my wakeup call, and sometimes, she'd have to pour buckets of water on me to wake me up. "You better get up. Your fans are waiting for you!" she'd scream, always doing some crazy shit to finally get me up.

As the song blew up, I had to keep going back to Germany. I was pretty much an overnight sensation. They gave me no time off. Everything started becoming a blur. Everything was disconnected. It just became one big memory, a constant rotation of flying, traveling, performing, doing interviews, getting in and out of cars and buses, and greeting fans. It all just blurred together.

Right after *Aaron's Party* released, I started doing my first concerts on my own. They were in Walmart parking lots to see if I could draw a crowd. Walmart promoted the concerts and Jive [*the record label*] ran them. The first show was in Halifax, Canada, and only like 500 people came to the show. They got really worried, but then, we went into America and pretty much every show sold out, except when I went into a big arena. It was empty, and I got pretty upset because I'd performed in front of full stadiums before, but that was opening for Britney Spears and the Backstreet Boys

I had to record music videos back to back, and they took me to Canada because you could work a kid longer hours there. Back to back to back, we recorded videos for "Aaron's Party," "Bounce, "Iko, Iko," and "I Want Candy." Four videos in three days. If you look at the "Aaron's Party" video, I have bags under my eyes like a sixty-year-old man. They kept me up forty-eight hours straight to shoot those videos. I fell asleep in the trailer every time we weren't shooting

My third album, *Oh Aaron*, was my least favorite. I was getting older—thirteen or fourteen years old—and each month felt like a year. I was growing up way too fast. The ages of twelve to fourteen felt like growing up in ten years, but by that point, I was a well-oiled machine, and it was just second nature working, touring, giving interviews. I just got used to it. I enjoyed it because of the fans. I got all the gratification and reassurance that I needed from them, but I wasn't getting it from my family.

It was like getting it from another family who I didn't even know.

I started realizing how alone I was in the world because nobody really knew me, not even my own family. I didn't even know myself. I was popular, but I didn't have an identity. What am I? Do I like making music? Am I good at it?

She [*I assume his mother*] hired a band of old, black funk musicians, and they really taught me how to be a musician, to play the piano. I couldn't identify with what I had been singing. It was all written by old guys, not what was coming from me. I was just portraying a fictitious story that someone else was telling.

ON MONEY

After that first concert, I got a record deal, but I have no idea how much it was for. I never saw any of it as far as I know. It all went to my parents' account. Fifteen percent was supposed to go into a trust per the law, but I never got it. When I turned eighteen, I received a little more than $2 million, but after over ten years of recording and touring, I was supposed to get a lot more.

♡

ON HIS ALBUMS

After the immediate success of "Crush on You" and performing in Germany, we went back to the States, to Pennsylvania, to start recording an album with Gary Carolla at his house. Gary started writing me songs, and Nick and Brian Littrell wrote me a song. We even recorded "Surfing in the USA" with NSYNC on the background.

After recording was done, it was back out on tour, doing it all over again. We were booking festivals, touring in Germany, and I was opening for the Backstreet Boys. I don't think I was even getting paid for that. It was just a promotion thing, but everybody saw a big payday if I got big. Everybody seemed to have their hand in the money that was being generated and made by me. At least, that's what I assume, but you never really know. I was nine or ten years old, so I had no idea what was going on.

I'm not bitter today because I wouldn't have what I have today if it wasn't for all those adults putting me out there. I don't look at my mom and dad any different because of it, no matter how much shit they did to me that was wrong. They sacrificed and gave up their dreams and jobs to help their kids have a career. Whether their intention was to help us or not doesn't matter. They did it. If I had kids and had them in show business, knowing what I know now, I'd protect them. But I could never do something that I considered beneath entertaining. I mean, I couldn't have a normal job, even if it means I have to suffer as an entertainer.

We did years of work to get that first album to become popular in the States. It was much more international, at least at first, but then, it broke big in England, and if you did that, it was like a welcome mat to America. I toured three years on that album, all over the world, doing thousands of shows. It went gold and platinum in probably like thirty or forty countries, enough to fill up all the walls in my house.

[*Writer's note: Aaron had tons of framed records and accomplishments in his house. When I was there, they were lined orderly along the floor, but he later showed me they had been hung professionally (I assume).*]

That's when I broke the Guinness Book of World Records for having four songs in the Billboard Top 100. [*Aaron is in the Guinness Book of World Records for being the youngest singer to have four consecutive top ten singles in the U.K.*] We only really did that album for like six months in America. About that time, I decided I would cut my hair off. I was tired of stewardesses telling my mom that she had a pretty girl.

Then, Jive signed me for a new album, and they flew me to New York to Battery Studios to record *Aaron's Party*. My mom and I lived in New York for a month, and I knocked the album out. Our agreement was that after every song I finished recording, she'd let me go on a spending spree. I was twelve years old, and my mom would hand me $10,000 in cash, and I'd go to the diamond district by myself and buy diamonds and gold watches. I was crazy over jewelry by this point.

[*There was something here about his brother not being able to do comedy skits in between songs on the album, so Wade Robson did them, pretending to be Nick, but I couldn't quite make it out.*]

Lou Pearlman was gone by this point. No one ever said anything to me about him. Just one day, he was gone, and I didn't ask. I found out later that my mom was suing him for $1,000,000.

I was the last person tied to Lou Pearlman before he was indicted. He knew the end was coming. I overheard him right before my eighteenth birthday say that he was quitting the business.

Recording that second album sucked. It was like boot camp. They forced me to go in the studio, and I had to finish the songs. The first album had been fun. Gary made it fun. It was entertaining for a little kid to do. We'd take breaks, go outside in the winter, and watch the deer lick salt bricks. Gary had a little farmhouse, and me and my mother stayed there while we recorded. In New York, when we recorded *Aaron's Party*, we stayed in some rental department in New York, but there was no difference between it and a hotel.

I remember my favorite thing to do was to get warm Krispy Kreme doughnuts. There was a store on the way to the studio, and I had to have them every morning. Mom didn't mind because it gave me energy. We'd go in that studio and boom, boom, boom, one song after another with no breaks. I didn't even know the songs until after I sang them. They just fed me lines, and I couldn't even remember the last lines that I sang. I didn't learn those songs until after recording. Sometimes, I didn't even know what I was saying. It sort of was like there was no creativity—just get in and do it, and do it right. There was lots of pressure on me. I was supposed to know what I was doing—"just get it right," they said.

The album was released in the United States and was a big success. Right before it released, I toured with

Britney Spears for the first album as a "brought on," where my team actually paid Britney to let me open for her to help my career. That was four or five months of touring with Britney, Monica, Destiny's Child and 98 Degrees and doing Nickelodeon Fest. Britney was like a big sister to me. I made her give me piggyback rides all the time. I never had a crush on her though, probably because she reminded me so much of my older sister BJ.

After that tour is when we did *Aaron's Party*, and it prepped me for touring in the States. Jive handled all that while my parents ran the show. At that point, I was already at the point of exhaustion. I didn't want to do it anymore. I just wanted to go do some normal kid stuff.

The family moved to Palos Verdes in California, and I told my mom I wanted to go back to school. "Okay," she said. "Let's give it a shot." I went for two weeks, but everyone knew me and would try to mess with me. I got in a fight with two kids who picked me up and threw me in a dumpster. [*Not sure who*] got knocked out with rollerblades. After that fight, I said to myself, "I guess I just can't live a normal life." I remember being really upset about that, and I kept to myself because I really couldn't express my emotions to anyone.

Almost all the conversations I had with my parents or anyone else was about music and business but never about money. My parents wouldn't allow me to ask about it. I'm not sure why, but my dad enforced that rule, and I didn't really wanna fuck with him.

I liked my fourth album, [*Another Earthquake!*], because I was doing more singing and taking it seriously. I still wasn't writing my own songs, but the material being picked was a lot more mature and cool. I liked the songs a lot more and felt like I was on the right path at that point. I was coming into my own and figuring out my identity, my look, seeing what I liked instead of what my parents wanted. I wanted to keep growing and evolving and to separate from anything I had done the year before.

♡

ON SUPPORTING HIS FAMILY FINANCIALLY

Once Nick was eighteen and took control of his money, I was the one giving my parents jobs. Before, Nick took care of the family, buying our houses and doing a great job supporting us. But after he turned eighteen, it was on me to keep my parents and everyone else working.

I was ten or eleven when I began to realize that I was the boss. I was the one employing my parents and all these people. It was my talent and hard work that was paying the bills. I was paying the rent. I remember when my dad realized I was the boss, he let me cut my hair. He finally caught on I was in charge. He didn't want me to be a singer—he wanted me to be a dirt bike racer.

When my second album came out, we toured so hard, it must have been thirty or forty countries, but by that point, I knew I was in charge. I was a showoff and did whatever I wanted. I would go around and just kick people in the balls and say to them, "What are you gonna do about it?" I was such a little shit. I became known for it. All the roadies and our employees like dancers and security guards and tutors would say, "Watch out—Aaron is going to kick you in the balls." That was the way I entertained myself as a child star.

All this time, I still was being taught how to sing, and it took forever for me to record anything. They'd feed me lines until the song was done. Sometimes, it would take ten hours.

As there was more fame and I got more popular, there was more money. We had bigger houses, more cars, everything started growing except for the relationships in the family. That was the sacrifice for all this stuff. The money started separating everyone even more.

Nick definitely took care of the family, adding to what I was making, but there was a point that he stopped giving so much money to the family because he was getting older and doing his own thing. He was there as long as he could until he felt he needed to go his own way. His work was paying for all that.

By fourteen or fifteen, I thought my parents should have more appreciation of the work he was putting in and answering his questions about how much he was making. They hid it from him, didn't want him to know how much it was.

Everybody around me was so scared of my mom and dad, but still, there were conversations with guardians that my parents didn't want me to have. They could fire these people whose livelihood was dependent on them. There were a lot of people on our payroll, and anyone working for the family had to be respectful or they'd get fired. And people got fired all the time. Bodyguards… all types of people got fired.

For one of my tours, my dad bought three buses, and then, he rented them back to me. It was his buddies from home that were driving the buses. There was a star coach for just me, the band, and crew and dancers and then two semis with the stage, gear, instruments, and a basketball and a basketball hoop, which was the most important thing to me when I was on tour.

ON GIRLS

I remember at my thirteenth birthday party, I had the pick of who I wanted as my girlfriend; Hilary Duff, Lindsay Lohan, and Mary Kate and Ashley showed up. I started dating Hilary Duff but probably had four or five girlfriends at a time. Amanda Bynes was my first girlfriend—I met her on tour. Hilary and I lost our virginity to each other at a hotel called *[unsure]* in LA. I think it was her birthday, maybe her thirteenth, but I don't remember. Her friends walked in, and we just yelled at them to get out.

I never dated any fans because my parents and bodyguards were around too much to let anything happen. Dating fans would have been too much of a liability.

ON HIS PARENTS

Mom and Dad became more distant, and I started noticing that my career was having a big impact on the longevity of my family. I began to foresee something bad was going to happen. Mom didn't care about being home. She was getting no affection, and I started to blame myself for them fighting so much. Alcohol was fueling a lot of the problems at home. My parents were giving up a lot of their lives for their kids with me and Nick touring, so when they got home, they would let loose. There were lots of highs and lows, almost bipolar.

We took extravagant vacations, went boating, private islands with the whole family but Nick. I really didn't see him for several years. He wasn't a big phone guy, but I remember getting in trouble racking up $500 and $600 international phone bills, though it was mostly calling my first girlfriend, this chick named Sara who was in a Swedish band called A-Teens.

I wasn't resentful of my parents, mostly because I got everything I wanted. I still didn't see any of the money I was earning except for a per diem, and I started saving that money up until it got to $20,000. Then, one time, my parents saw it in an airport in the Philippines and took the money. It was a bunch of cash from different countries in this backpack that I carried around. The only things in it were the cash, Beanie Babies [*Aaron loved his Beanie Babies*], and Swatch watches. I would use my per diem to buy Game Boys, watches, laptops because I wanted different colors in the new versions, dirt bikes, whatever I wanted.

After my fourth album, I was getting done with all this, and I could tell my family was about to be done too. We never had a break.

I remember I was working during Christmas on a Disney cruise ship when I was fifteen. Lindsay Lohan was my girlfriend at the time, and she was on the cruise ship too. Right before I left, my mom asked me if she should divorce my dad. I said, "Yeah, you guys aren't getting along," but really, I just wanted to be able to get away with more. But I didn't take it seriously. My mom said, "Okay."

I did the cruise, both parents went on it, and when we got back home to the Keys, *MTV Cribs* came to the house to film that episode. Ten minutes before we started filming, my guardian and background singer told me that my parents' divorce was final and that after the *Cribs* episode, I'd have to go pack my stuff up and move with my mom to a house she'd bought in Parkland. I was like, "Oh my gosh, I have to do this episode now?"

In the back of my head, I was thinking I shouldn't be doing this. It was a weird way of saying goodbye to my life down there, but I always went with my mom. She was always there, but both parents were distant and separate, so by this point, I was running around, sneaking drinks and hitting on girls, being reckless, making out with girls.

After we moved to Parkland, my mom wanted me to get back at it with no break. I remember her being reckless and drinking a lot to where it was scaring me, and I didn't wanna be there. She'd bought that house in Parkland with my money. A $2 million house she pulled out of my trust fund. I was supposed to get the house but didn't because I left my mom.

I remember on my fifteenth birthday, I was really sick with the flu and some business manager my mom had got me a G Wagon for my birthday. This business manager had me sign some paperwork for it. I remember my mom wasn't even taking care of me even though I was sick—I was in the guesthouse alone while Mom and BJ were in the main house. They came in when I was sick and had me sign something. I remember my mom didn't even acknowledge I was sick. I would just sit in that guesthouse with my three dogs and hang out with them, watching the same DVDs over and over. I did have a four-wheeler, but there really wasn't any place to ride it.

On my birthday, when I went to tell my mom I was sick, she was in the house, drunk with some cop. I told her I didn't want to be there, I wanted to be in the Keys, and this guy started yelling at me. I was like, "Yo, you can't yell at me. My dad will come up here and kill you." I was going to take my G Wagon and drive to the Keys to get my dad even though I didn't have a license, but they took my key and threw it in the water. I ended up jumping the gate and walking a few miles down the road, calling a friend from a payphone, and he drove me to my dad's in the Keys. My dad let me have the break from entertainment that I wanted, and I took a year off.

Later, my dad told me that when I thought I was signing for that G Wagon, I was actually signing over the house to my mom. But I don't know if that was true because they were always trying to blame each other. But I never got any money for that house.

The house in the Keys was in Marathon, and there were like fifteen houses on the property. Me and Nick paid for it. It was walled off with trees and gates and guarded by Rottweilers and Dobermans. You could take golf carts everywhere. Each kid had their own house on the compound.

♡

ON DRUGS

The first person I ever smoked weed with was my older sister BJ. Drinking was never really my thing.

I spent $30,000 one summer on ecstasy when I was fifteen. My dad would pass out drunk, and I would take his Escalade and illegally drive two hours to Miami, where I would meet this shirtless Cuban drug dealer who always had a gun in his waistband.

One time, I went to buy a pound of weed through one of the Cuban's connects and went to a Miami Subs to buy it. I brought it back to the Keys and sold the weed and some of the ecstasy. My parents had no idea I was doing this, and in fact, they still don't. "Hi, Mom, sorry to tell you about this."

I would buy thirty or forty ecstasy pills at a time, then bring it back to my house and feed it to everybody. We'd have vapor rub parties and stay up all night, listening to music.

One time, my dad found a pound of weed in my safe. I don't know how he was able to crack into it. I don't know if he had hidden cameras or how he got the code, but when I came home, the safe was open, the weed was gone, and I knew it was my dad. I avoided him for four or five days until he came up to me and said, "You hiding from me? Have anything you want to tell me?"

I said, "Can I have it back?"

He said, "You're not using this for personal use."

I said, "Yes, I am. Besides, you were known for being a drug dealer back in your hometown in New York."

My dad just kept the weed on him and would give it to me to smoke sometimes when he was drinking. My parents knew I smoked weed and were lenient about it, but that was the first time I got caught. My dad knew before though because a friend had taken pictures of me smoking weed and sold them to the *National Enquirer*. I was fifteen years old when I was on the front page, smoking weed. I was on tour when it came out a few months later.

We knew this Cuban named Ramon [*unsure who called who*] "Puta" in the Keys, and then he moved with us to Orlando. I asked him for some coke once, and he kept calling it *perico*, but it was heroin. I snorted it, and it was heroin, and it was the best feeling I ever felt. I rode a scooter back to the house and had the most incredible experience, but then I got sick for two days, and that's when I stopped putting anything up my nose. I even did it on the plane once.

THE KEYS

I just wanted to party and basically live in my own house and do whatever I wanted. That's when I started getting in trouble and being reckless. I got alcohol poisoning multiple times, and that was when I was first introduced to Xanax. I would take four or five bars and get blacked out. My dad was usually passed out, and besides, he had control over the town and the cops.

I had a local drug dealer and [*I believe he was referring to himself*] always had a mob with [*me*], the baddest kids in town always surrounding [*me*]. I was never alone. No one would fuck with me.

I made friends down there through my dad, who would meet people in the water. He would find friends for me, guys who were into smoking weed and drinking and shark fishing late at night on the boats.

My best friend in the Keys was a guy named Craig. When I got older, I distanced myself from Craig, but for a while, he'd go on tour with me. His parents even pulled him out of school, and he did home school with me. We were dickheads to the boy dancers and would fuck with the tutor. We would flip him in shark-infested waters (haha). We tormented him so badly, he quit and moved to Egypt.

We would go deep sea fishing with Craig's dad super early in the morning. His name was Earl, but we called him Early Man, and his mom was Terri Jo [*unsure of spelling*]. They were the closest thing to family and normal life for me once the family business had started. We'd take our catches to restaurants, and they'd cook it for us. I remember one was called Castaways. We'd go out on fishing tours, and there wasn't much to do but fish. We drank behind our parents' backs and went to parties.

Craig and I started growing apart as he was busy doing marine stuff—renting boats and jet skis and that type of stuff. His house was a mile from the Seven Mile Bridge, and we were both little rich kids with fast boats, snorkeling, spearfishing. Everybody wanted to hang out with us. Craig never really seemed to care that I was famous, and he never needed anything from me. In fact, he had all the shit I wanted: boats and stuff. I started getting in trouble with other kids, but I just wanted time off, really just to party and enjoy my money and fame and wealth. I was spent.

I wasn't talking to my mom too much. Then, she tried to get my dad back. This was after I left Parkland. She showed up and snuck onto the property and walked into the Cuban House where I was playing beer pong and was like, "Aha, I caught you!" I didn't care. Then, she left and headed toward the main house where my dad was with the woman he ended up marrying, Ginger. I knew what was going to happen.

I heard breaking glass and ran to the white house and saw all this shattered glass on the ground. Ginger was naked, and my mom was beating her up. My dad was like, "Help me!" but we couldn't calm her down. Next thing I knew, Ginger was knocked out. I'm the one that called the cops, and my mom got arrested, and then I bailed her out. I wish I hadn't [*called the cops*] because maybe they would have gotten back together if I hadn't. My mom was just so sad and upset.

When the cops came, Ginger was hiding upstairs, and the cops went to question her. She had marks, mostly on her nose and forehead. My dad was just quiet, in shock probably, trying to figure out what to do. I just left. I'd just turned sixteen and had my license and got in my G Wagon and drove away with $1,500 in cash. I usually had $50,000 or $60,000 in cash on me, mostly from per diem they'd give me and I'd squirrel away. They'd give me like $500 a week, but there was always catering that I would eat.

I didn't work at all from the ages of sixteen to seventeen. Just hung out, boating, partying, throwing house parties, dating every girl in town, and pissing off people's boyfriends.

ON NICK AND THE BACKSTREET BOYS

I wanted to sound like all the guys in the Backstreet Boys together. They were all so talented, and I looked up to each of them individually.

I was everybody's little brother in the Backstreet Boys. They all loved me. I was always running around, just hanging out with them. All the little sisters of the fans of the Backstreet Boys became my fans, and in many households, the older kids had Backstreet Boys posters on the wall and the younger kids had Aaron Carter posters.

Nick was very encouraging, and he taught me a lot. He always challenged me to be a better singer. I had great admiration for my brother and his abilities as a singer and performer. I used to get chills when he hit high notes and angelic tones. Eventually, I wanted to grow into sounding like him but also like the other guys in his band too. I studied each of them, but I really didn't sing until my fourth album—it was more like kiddy rapping before that. But I wanted to be a singer, not a rapper.

When Nick was living in Florida, he would go to LA to do some movies, and I would stay with him in Beverly Hills. I would always be excited to see Nick. He was always a good big brother. Andrew [*unsure which Andrew*], who was my good friend from before, became friends with Nick and started living with him. I thought that was a little annoying because Andrew was my friend. Then, all of a sudden, Nick and Andrew are living together.

It wasn't too exciting when we were out there, though I remember coming back to Nick's house when he was dating Paris Hilton, and I found a wrapper with coke in it, and I did it by myself even though I was alone. I assumed it was hers. She was always at the house. Nick was getting caught up in the Paris scene, but he would never get me any weed or anything. But I would go to the club with them.

Paris and Nicole had *The Simple Life* show at that point. Nicole was always flirtatious. I think she wished I was older, but I never hooked up with her. I didn't really get caught up in the star fucking. I always wanted to be the most famous person in the group. Any other famous people, I didn't fuck with because I wanted to be the most famous. That's why I was drug dealing. I wasn't interested in hanging with other people in the industry. Can't be a snitch—not street code.

♡

ON GOING BACK TO WORK

After taking time off living in the Keys with my dad, just partying and boating and not working, I turned seventeen and my dad said it was time to go back to work. He sold the property in the Keys, and we moved to Orlando to be closer to Lou [*Pearlman*] so I could start working again.

There still was an existing $1,000,000 judgment against Lou, but my dad signed some deal with Lou and wiped it away. Lou gave me like $30,000 in cash and my dad $50,000, and then, on my seventeenth birthday, Lou gave me a bright red Viper truck with a stick shift. When he gave it to me, Lou told everyone to go outside, and I could tell he was really excited that he was back with me, since the Backstreet Boys and Britney and NSYNC wouldn't touch him anymore. We did one song called "Saturday Night," and it did great, and then I started going back on tour.

I started dating one of my dancers named Brittany, and it was the first time that I was allowed to date one of my dancers and be on the road together. We got into cocaine real bad. We'd be on stage with the other kids, super high. I'd tried it once or twice before, but I felt like I was going to die. When I was touring, it felt again like I was back in that monotonous, repetitive pattern with only one new song.

ON TURNING EIGHTEEN

My eighteenth birthday was approaching. That was when all the money that I had made over the past decade plus should be mine. It turned out I was getting a little over $2 million, but Leslie once showed me my trust fund paperwork, and it had over $6 million in it. I guess my parents would get judges to release it early, but by this time, I had quit the business again and was getting scared as my birthday got closer. I just didn't understand how much money I had or what was going on. It didn't make sense to me, but I never really knew how much I was making. I trusted my dad, but he was really greedy with money.

Then, on my eighteenth birthday, we went to the Bank of America in Orlando to get my money. I remember waking up very excited, almost like Christmas morning, but the day ended horribly. I forged my mom's signature and got a card with almost $3 million on it. We drove home, and my dad started drinking Crown and Diet Cokes. He started demanding that I pay him money for back management commissions I owed him. He said he wanted 10 percent to 20 percent in back commissions. I told him no, I wasn't giving him the money, and he ended up attacking me and forcing me to sign a check. He picked me up and threw me on the ground, then pulled out a .44 magnum and shot it at a tree close to my ear. That's a powerful and loud gun, and it exploded my eardrum. My ear was bleeding, so I signed over a check to my dad for $280,000.

I just wanted to leave, to get out of there, so I called my friend Steven from the Keys, and he drove up to Orlando to pick me up. I got in the car with him and left all my stuff at my dad's place in Orlando. Steven took me to The Mall at Millenia, where I was eyeing this piece of jewelry that cost $80,000, a cross necklace with eighteen diamonds in the cross. [*Not sure if he bought it, but I believe he said he did.*]

Steven and I stayed in a hotel in Orlando that night, and the next day, I went house shopping in some place called Howey-in-the-Hills. I called the realtor and then went to look at the house but thought it might be boring and decided I wanted to leave Florida. So, instead, I booked a flight to Amsterdam [*I'm not exactly clear who was on this trip.*] My sister BJ went with me, along with her boyfriend named Wes who became like a brother to me. We stayed at a nice place in the heart of the red-light district and enjoyed the area. I'd been there before as a kid for shows but had never really experienced it. It was cool going back to Amsterdam and starting my own adventures as an adult.

But I ruined the whole trip because the first day, we stumbled across mushrooms, and I took too many. I was all alone tripping, talking to the bathtub, watching the curtains, and having all these emotional highs and lows, seeing everything from rainbows to lightning. I always overdid everything. I took some blue minis and philosopher stones and ate a whole chocolate bar, but everyone else took a fraction of what I took.

LOS ANGELES

[*Writer's's note: This was after he was eighteen. I'm not sure how long after, but he still had the millions from the money that was turned over to him on his eighteenth birthday.*]

Me and BJ got on a plane and landed in LA. We went right to the Palazzo, one of the nicest apartment buildings in town, and got the penthouse. We got the keys, moved in, then I went to Mercedes and bought a white CLS500. Then, we went to the rim shop, then to Guitar Center. I wanted to learn to make my own beats. I wanted to produce. I spent half a million dollars there. I bought an SSL AWS900 console/mixing board, an MPC2500, a Yamaha Motif ES8 keyboard, 16-20 outboard gears, rolling speakers, guitars, and a C8800 microphone. They knew who I was and definitely upsold me, but I was clueless and just said, "Give me the best stuff." I just wanted to learn to make beats. The guys from the store set it up, but they didn't show me how to use it.

Wes, BJ's boyfriend, encouraged me. He had a friend named Zach Horn [*unsure of spelling*], and I started paying Zach to show me how to make beats in a loop and structure the songs. I was interested in my own music theory, and I've been doing that now for years.

I became a musician when I got to LA. I took it very seriously. Industry people and family members made fun of me, but that would just make me want to do better. All those guys helped teach me a lot. Zach was purposefully holding stuff back because, if not, he'd be out of a job.

Even though Nick never apologized for that *House of Carters* episode, we sent him some of my beats, and he wanted to buy the "Fool's Gold" song from me, and I said no. To me, that was the ultimate validation.

It was like going to school. I was paying for my own college. I lived in Hollywood but didn't go to clubs or go out. I just worked nonstop on my music. It was my way of feeling gratification, hearing something I'd finished and created. I created more and more beats, but nothing happened with them. I used to create beats based on who it would sound good for and eventually created my own music theory. It was important to me to create my own body of work so I could be a real artist.

I did that for a few years but started to run out of money. If I had been smarter, it would have lasted longer, but I bought all of Pharrell's ice cream shoes, trunks at Louis Vuitton. I got an Escalade, a Viper. The penthouse was three bedrooms, and rent was $5,500 a month, and all three of my sisters were living with me on and off. We were right off 3rd Street across from the Grove in a four-floor building with not one thing on the wall the whole time we lived there. I just didn't care about that stuff. All I cared about was weed, music, cars, and clothes. I didn't even give a shit about girls. How could I with three sisters living there? I never once even brought a girl back. I would just try to hook up with their friends.

One of the few times I did go to the club when I lived in LA, I got punched in the face at Element. The guy ripped off the $100,000 necklace I was wearing and ran out of the club and jumped in a car. They knew who I was when I walked in there. I was wearing cowboy boots and a fur coat. Everyone saw what happened and followed the guy out. We called the cops and filed a police report, and a week later, a detective we hired found the necklace at a pawn shop. We pressed charges, and I think the guy got four years.

Eventually, we had to move out in the valley because I was out of money. I lived with a girlfriend named Casey [*unsure of spelling*] [*unclear if Aaron was still supporting sisters*], and I was paying for everything from weed to food to clothing. I paid for everything, but I didn't mind.

Then, I set up some recording sessions in San Francisco with AP.9, a gangster rapper, through Zach and Wes.

[*Writer's's note: It is difficult to follow the story here, but it seems another rapper who had a street beef with AP.9 whom Aaron did not want to name set up AP.9's house to get robbed. I believe Aaron's recording equipment and some jewelry was stolen. Aaron said he told AP.9 he was going to have the thief killed and called gangsters he knew in other states, one of whom offered to do it for three grand. Aaron said he'd double it. But when his twin sister, Angel, overheard the conversation, he dropped it. "If she hadn't been standing there, I would have gone through with it," he said.*]

I asked for Detective Jarvis, the same detective who got my necklace back, and he told me, "We got a lead on who did this, but it's in your best interest to drop it so you don't have to look over your shoulder for the rest of your life." Ever since then, I've always brought all my jewelry with me wherever I go.

ORLANDO

I was finally out of money, so I moved to Orlando and started dating some girl named Sage who was some billionaire's daughter. I sold my Mercedes, sold my Viper, and started to get into Xanax really bad. Sage and I started getting into fights where the cops were called. She was talking to her ex behind my back.

Eventually, I called Nick and told him I was having a hard time and asked him for help. Nick invited me to go on tour in the northwest and Canada with him, just to hang out and be mentored by him. He started giving me positive thinking books. I was twenty-one or twenty-two years old, and everyone was like, "Let's get Aaron in a positive place."

All the guys in Backstreet Boys were like brothers to me. Brothers I didn't really know that well, but that wasn't unlike my own brother. Nick's bodyguard named Q, who passed away, really took me under his wing. Q was like a big brother to me. He told me he loved me and that I would get through this and that I needed to listen to my brother. I was going to do the same things that they did to change Nick when he got his act together. Nick wanted to help get me where he was and do it faster than it had happened for him, which put a lot of pressure on me.

It was all the same [*Backstreet Boys*] crew as from when I was a kid because they were like a family. So, all these people on tour knew me from when I was a kid.

I was depressed and really skinny, and they were all worried about me. After the tour ended, I moved into Nick's guesthouse in Tennessee and started working on beats there. I started going to a trainer, but I was still getting Xanax from people. The first thing Nick did was make me go to the doctor where I was diagnosed with a [*hiatal, I believe*] hernia, which is an old man's stress disease. They said I had to change my diet and start going to the gym, and Nick was forcing vitamins and healthy stuff down my throat, but I didn't want to do it. I just wanted to sleep and smoke weed. I'd just lost all my money, I had no girl, I wasn't touring, I wasn't singing. I was just making beats to keep me feeling like I accomplished something in life.

Nick was trying to help me get healthy and live a healthy lifestyle. He also tried to hook me up with Andrew Fromm, a talented songwriter and neighbor of his, but he was more interested in creating his own music.

That's not who I was. I didn't want to play other people's music anymore; I wanted something a lot more personal. I knew my music sucked, but it didn't stop me from wanting to do better.

I just started being really reclusive. I'd had to sell all my equipment and was just using a laptop to make my beats, but nothing was going on. This was around 2009, and I got myself a Twitter account, and I started the hashtag #AARONCARTERCELL and released my cell phone number. I sat in Nick's guesthouse for probably four or five months, just picking up the phone thousands of times a day with all the calls and texts from fans. I just wanted to see if I still had these legions of fans.

I created a journal and logged where everyone was from, how old they were. I wanted to get statistics and know my fans' demographics. What better way than to ask people directly by getting thousands of calls a day. I filled up that journal, mostly because I was bored. That caused a buzz, and I had nothing else going on. I was just taking a lot of Xanax and being bored.

Then, one day, I got a call from ABC. They wanted me to be on *Dancing with the Stars*. I had no money, and that was a big paycheck. I didn't realize it, but I had been offered *Dancing with the Stars* before, but now, I needed the money. I thought, *I should do this. Maybe I have a chance of winning.* I booked it and had a couple of months before shooting, so I started to train. I didn't lay off the weed or Xanax while training, but I did go to a facility called D1 in Tennessee for training camp before shooting started. *Dancing with the Stars* put me up in the Palazzo again and gave me a rental car and gave me a very big check. I think it was for like 300 or 400 grand. I did the competition and got some notoriety again, and I got all my confidence back.

That time in Tennessee was very helpful to me, and I feel bad that I've never properly thanked Nick and still haven't to this day. But I did *Dancing with the Stars,* and it was a great experience. One of the hardest things I've ever done—the grind, the packages, the promos, the eight-hour rehearsal days. Karina Smirnoff ended up breaking up with her fiancé during the show for me. Plus, her and I had other issues, and then we started talking and getting more intimate and spending time together outside of rehearsals. I let her know she was too much for me, and she agreed, and we started resenting each other in the midst of the competition, and we started having to rehearse with different people because our relationship was so bad. We reached the top five, then the shit hit the fan personally, and we were voted out of the fifth spot.

After the show, I thought my career was back and I would move back to LA, but that didn't happen. Instead, everything abruptly stopped. There were no offers for TV shows or any agents booking concerts, and that had been the main reason I did the show—to announce to the world, "Hey, I'm still here." But it didn't happen.

I still had some *Dancing with the Stars* money left, so I moved into a different apartment in LA. I remember that year I was there alone for Christmas, and I got in a road rage incident. I was still taking a lot of Xanax, and I wasn't talking to anyone in the family. I was pissed at everyone, but I was the one being the dick. I resented everyone for the divorce. I felt like the other siblings didn't care, and I was hitting another big depression. I had nothing going on except some charity events.

♡

MIAMI

In 2011 or so, I decided to move to Miami. I didn't have any connections or relationships there that would get me to perform, and it wasn't really close to family, but for some reason, it's where I wanted to be.

I hadn't done any shows in forever, and I was starting to miss performing. I started to think, *How do I get back into it and do music again?* Then, I started dating a girl named Mylie [*unsure of spelling*] who was a dancer in Orlando. I wanted to be closer to her, so she moved in with me into a beautiful new high-rise apartment in downtown Brickell. I still had a couple hundred grand left but was so careless with money, I wasn't even thinking about it. I just wanted to show off for this girl, I guess.

But we weren't even getting along. Fighting a lot, but still, we got engaged. I was taking so much Xanax that I don't even remember the ring, but I know that I *[later, he said she]* threw it off our balcony, a $15,000 ring. I do remember I drove up to her parents' house in Orlando to ask for permission to marry her. I wasn't nervous to propose. I didn't even know why I was doing it because

I didn't actually want to marry her. It was more like I was yearning for what I thought was normal. I didn't even plan the proposal. When we went to the movies to watch *Alice in Wonderland*, in the middle of the movie, I just handed her the ring. It was like, "Look, will you marry me?" She said, "Absolutely!"

After that, everything got real. She got pregnant, and we both agreed to have an abortion. I realized this wasn't what I wanted to do, and we shouldn't do it [*I am unsure whether he is referring to the abortion or marriage*] and told her I wasn't ready for it. We kept having dumb disagreements, and everything kept building up, and it ended up not working.

The night I told her, she acted like she was gonna jump off the balcony like forty floors up. I had to grab her, and it was a real scary situation. She got in her car and drove to Orlando, and I threw all her shit out. Anything that had remnants of her, I threw in the dumpster.

I ran into her in LA a few years later, and she was pregnant.

BACK TO ORLANDO

After being in Miami and breaking up with my girl, I was out of money again. I started to get lonely. Then, Johnny Wright, who had been working with Timberlake, reached out to me when I was doing *Dancing with the Stars* and said he wanted to manage me. I was like, "Oh shit!" Yeah, this is the perfect time.

Johnny lived in Florida and had a music compound in Orlando where I could go live and make beats. When I was moving from Miami, me and Jayson Sanchez got in a fight while moving and packing everything into a U-Haul. Jayson was wheeling out this big eight-foot glass table, and I told him to chill, but he disregarded me again and went in front of me, and the glass table fell and broke and cut Jayson's artery. There was blood everywhere. He was dying. I tied a tourniquet while waiting for 911 and even stuck my thumb in his arm. I never saw blood like that before. He was the color of blue and gray. I think he bled like half of the seven pints of blood we have in our body. I escorted him into the ambulance and left the hospital and went back to packing.

When I got to Orlando, I checked in at Johnny Wright's compound. Everyone had been there. It was on a lake with a basketball court and volleyball court. It's a Mediterranean-looking house but all wood. Rustic, a little beat down though, with the smell of old water. My room was a shitty little room with two beds against a wall with a small TV from the '90s. There was another room with a pool table, but it felt like it was haunted. It gave off this negative energy.

My beats were terrible then. I can look back at beats and remember where I was when I created them. I worked with a bunch of people at Johnny's compound and cut some songs. I was taking more Xanax at that point than ever before, at least six milligrams a day, all during recording. Johnny started inviting execs and A&R people to come listen, and everyone told them, "No, Aaron Carter can never be again. It's not going to work for him." Steve Rifkind from Interscope shunned me when he was at the compound—he didn't even acknowledge me. I figured it was because of my songs, not who I was, at least that's what I kept telling myself so I would think there was still some hope.

I stayed at the compound a little longer until Christmastime, but I was out of control with drinking red wine and taking Xanax. Christmas had always been horrible for me after the divorce. I remember emailing Johnny from inside the compound—he was in his own house—and telling him I wasn't doing good. I called my mom, and she drove over from Tampa and got me. I was on the phone with Nick, and we basically had an intervention for me. Johnny, Jayson [*Sanchez, I assume*], Nick was on the phone, Angela the assistant, Doug Brown was there, the property caretakers were there, but I was doing all the talking at the intervention. I felt like I'd set up my own intervention. Then, Nick paid for me to go to the Betty Ford Center in Palm Desert.

My mom took me to Tampa, then to rehab. I remember taking my last Xanax before getting on the plane. Nick picked us up in LA, and the three of us drove to rehab. I checked in under the name Chaz Spalding and was there for thirty days. Nick wanted me to do ninety days. I completed it, but I got one Xanax halfway through from another patient.

I was lonely and didn't like the process. I had to get up at 5:00 in the morning to do some weird-ass chant. There were same-sex houses, and I couldn't even have a conversation with the opposite sex. It was boring.

I started getting my head together but wanted to smoke weed but not take Xanax. I finished rehab and went back to the compound in Orlando. I expected there to be a support system there, but there was nothing ready for me, no family there. Four months went by, and I was back in the same room, completely sober with no friends or family there and this moldy smelling house.

Johnny didn't have anything for me and told me no one wants to do anything with me, so I left and went out to California to Orange County with [*I believe he is referring to Jayson Sanchez here*] and his parents, staying in his little brother's room, hoping something was going to come up. I started smoking weed again and started abusing Unisom, which is just like Xanax. I took it to sleep at first because when I'm sober, I can't sleep, but it was really just a cheat to quitting Xanax.

NEW YORK

I was broke, and then I got an opportunity out of nowhere to do a play in New York, off Broadway. It wasn't the biggest paying thing, but it was more about the credibility. I ended up auditioning for The Fantasticks but didn't get it—they said I wasn't good enough. I asked for notes, then tried it one more time, and this time, they saw something they liked, so I booked the job with a residency in New York City. I moved to New York with only a suitcase and started rehearsing five days before opening night. I was the lead, the costar with a love interest. Matt Leisy was leaving, and I was replacing him, but he was great. I studied him.

Before I knew it, it was opening night. I didn't think I was going to be able to do it, but I memorized a million lines—all I did in my apartment was memorize. I got through that first night and surprised everyone. I wasn't making great money, but they put me up in great buildings.

Before I got there, no one was coming, but on my opening night, they sold out, with people coming from all over the world to see me. After the show, I had to go out and mingle with the audience, which the cast wasn't used to, though they deserved to do it. That cast was a beautiful family of talented people that I became a part of. I realized again just how many fans I had.

Robert Felstein was the pianist and music director, and one day, he took me aside and told me I sounded like shit. He said that everyone was making fun of me on my stage and that I sounded like a pop singer, not a classic singer. This guy just laid into me, threatened to fire me if I didn't quit smoking and start singing better. I looked terrible when I started, but I knew I couldn't lose that job, so I spent all my time practicing and doing eight shows a week.

Then, halfway through the show, the IRS came after me for $7 million for taxes my parents never paid. My bank account and wages got garnished, and I had to live on $180 a week. I started drinking whiskey, Jameson neat, at a sushi bar. I had to find $1,500 for a bankruptcy attorney and was just hoping for a series 7, but I couldn't pay the attorneys. When I asked my parents and siblings, no one would give me any money—I just needed $1,500 more, but they said, "No, you need to do it on your own." I was praying that I could go back on tour, praying to

God. I was done doing The Fantasticks and didn't want to be there anymore.

I was hoping something was going to come out of thin air when an agent named Alex Ross and Matt Raffle [*unclear who this is*] went to my show. I was nailing it, and after the show, Alex was waiting for me in the lobby and told me, "I think we should put you on tour." I told him I'd been praying for that and that I would love that. A week later, I put in my resignation for The Fantasticks, and they [*I assume Alex and Matt*] gave me $20,000. It was like hitting the lottery.

ON HIS MENTAL HEALTH

Making beats saved my life. I was always suicidal, especially through those years. I never attempted suicide but never had anyone to talk to about it. But I knew I loved life too much to actually do it. Hopefully I won't do it. All I wanted was to have my own family since I lost my own family. That would be the best feeling. That's what happened for Nick, and it changed his whole life around. Losing my family was really impactful.

THE END

EPILOGUE

I last spoke with Aaron in April of 2021. "Hey man heading to LA for the next week if you want to get the book going again," I texted. I recall not having high hopes; he'd been difficult to tie down recently.

"What's up my brother!!!!! Let's get it going," he wrote. Then: "I'm with it!! Our iron is hottttt right now."

We never got together that trip.

I next texted him after his celebrity boxing match with Lamar Odom that June. "Hey man, impressed with the fight. That's a big dude and you held your own, showed no fear. That'll be a chapter in the book!"

He never responded.

My final text to Aaron would be on November 24, 2021, just after his son Prince was born. Knowing how much he wanted children and his own family, I was beyond excited for him. "Congrats man! Life changing, isn't it? I think it's time to get the book going again. Perfect life event to show your growth."

Unfortunately, we never did get the book going again. We never had a chance to talk about him relapsing or meeting Melanie or the birth of his son. There was a lot we never talked about. But there was a lot we did, and I recounted it the best I could with the information Aaron provided me.

Aaron, I'm sorry we didn't get to talk more about your issues, your addiction, your state of mind. I can't help but think if we had finished this book, if I had pushed you more, if I had been more focused on it, that it would have helped you heal. That maybe, just maybe, telling your story to the world would have given you the peace you were always looking for.

Well, here it is.

—Andy Symonds

ABOUT THE AUTHORS

Pop sensation Aaron Carter rose to international stardom in the '90s and 2000s, selling millions of albums and performing before sold-out stadiums around the world, following in the footsteps of his older brother, Nick Carter of the Backstreet Boys. Aaron's life and career were equally derailed by family conflicts, drug addiction, and mental health challenges. Nonetheless, he remained dedicated to his art and continued to create music until his tragic death on Nov. 5, 2022.

Andy Symonds is the author and editor of dozens of books, including *My Father's Son, The Man in the Arena,* and the forthcoming *Reality Check.* He is also the founder and CEO of Ballast Books and Blue Balloon Books.

Printed in Great Britain
by Amazon